WITHDRAWN

HEINRICH von KLEIST

AMPHITRYON

A Comedy

Translated from the German,
with an introduction, by
MARION SONNENFELD
Assistant Professor of German
Smith College

FREDERICK UNGAR PUBLISHING CO.
NEW YORK

To
Kurt and Sibylla Sonnenfeld
with all my gratitude and love

PREFACE

With great idealism and high hopes the translator of a work
of genius approaches his task. As he sets to work he seeks to
convey content, thought and a flavor of style within the form
of the original. He is so delighted with the original work and
feels privileged to be able to transmit it to others.

As he continues his work, he realizes full well that he is
doomed to partial failure. He is not the original creator; he
is not shaping both language and content to each other; he
can only hope to convey plot and thought, and, in so doing,
pray that he is not destroying style completely. And, worst
of all, the intimacy with the original, the chance to study it
word for word, inevitably increases his appreciation of its
excellence.

Having had this experience with *Amphitryon*, I humbly offer
it to the reader. I hope that you will still find Kleist in most
of these words. And I also hope that you will enjoy your reading,
especially wherever he does come through.

M.S.

INTRODUCTION

I

Bernd Wilhelm Heinrich von Kleist was born in Frankfurt-on-Oder in 1777, the son of the retired Major Joachim Friedrich von Kleist and the latter's second wife, Juliane von Pannwitz. By the time young Kleist was sixteen, he had lost both his parents. His best friends were the theologian Christian Ernst Martini and his stepsister Ulrike von Kleist. His close relationship with his sister was to continue throughout the rest of his life.

Kleist had entered the Prussian army in 1792, served in the Rhine campaign of 1796 and retired from the army as a lieutenant in 1799. He considered the army years lost time and explained in a letter to Martini that the army was not for him, because a man cannot live in steady conflict with himself. As a human being, one wants to act in one way; as an officer, one has to obey orders. Raising a problem which later confronts his Amphitryon, Kleist asked: "Can there be a situation in which a rational being should put more trust in the convictions of another man than he puts in his own?"

When he was asked what plans he had for earning his living, Kleist became most disdainful. He chose to study mathematics, physics, philosophy and law. To Martini he wrote that the day laborer leads a truly idyllic life; to be sure, "deprivation and poverty surround him; his whole life seems to be nothing but eternal worry, work, and deprivation. But contentment shines from his eyes; joy smiles from his face . . ." Kleist goes on to define happiness: "I call those rich and abundant enjoyments which we derive from the contemplation of our own moral beauty, happiness." The whole person, at one with himself, as Alkmene before the start of *Amphitryon,* is then a happy person.

In a letter to his sister in 1799 young Kleist discussed another of his key ideas: everyone must make himself a detailed plan of what he wants to achieve in life and then live in accordance with it. He himself, however, and, mirroring his experience, his dramatic figures, had to learn that one can never carry out rigid personal plans without outside interference.

In Frankfurt, Kleist met young Wilhelmine von Zenge who soon became his fiancée. His correspondence with her has been partially preserved, and it reads like an amazing document of torture and self-torture. For Kleist tries to undertake to educate and form his bride, to correct her grammar and style, and to pose problems to her on which she is to write essays. These he will read, correct, and criticize, "for through written solution of interesting problems," he informs her in 1800," we do not merely practice the application of grammar and style but also the use of our higher intellectual faculties, and finally our judgment on doubtful subjects will be determined and we ourselves will gradually be enriched by some interesting truths."

Much has been said and written about the trip to Würzburg that Kleist made in 1800. Some think that he was on a government mission, for he was about to enter government service at the time; others claim that Kleist, having learned that Wilhelmine was eager to have children, took the trip to undergo a needed operation to make him capable of fatherhood; a third theory is that Kleist went to Würzburg to undergo a cure for venereal disease. It does seem clear from his letters, especially from one which describes the Julius Hospital in Würzburg in great detail, that he was hospitalized there. In another letter he expressed his uncertainty about Wilhelmine's steadfastness: ". . . You are only a weak girl after all; and my inexplicable trip, this separation of weeks', perhaps months', duration . . . oh God, suppose you were to get sick! Dear, beloved, faithful girl! Be a strong girl, too! Trust me completely! Stake all your happiness on my sincerity!"

After the stay in Würzburg, he did enter government service in Berlin. And now came what some critics have called the decisive encounter of Kleist's life; he began to read the philosopher Kant. He did not completely understand the *Critique of Knowledge*, but felt almost shattered by it. He wrote similarly to both Ulrike and Wilhelmine about this experience:

"It seems that I shall become another of the many victims of folly whom Kantian philosophy has on its conscience. I abhor this company, and yet I cannot wrest myself from its chains. The idea that we can know nothing, nothing at all, about truth in this life; that what we call truth here is something else after death; and that, as a result, striving to attain property which will follow us to the grave is totally in vain and fruitless; these thoughts have upset me in the very sanctity of my soul. My sole and highest aim has vanished, I no longer have one. Since then, I abhor books, I put my hands in my lap and look for a new goal which my intellect could happily strive to approach. But I cannot find it, and inner restlessness drives me about. I run to cafés and tobacco shops, to concerts and plays; I commit follies which I am ashamed to put down on paper, all in the hope of diverting myself. And still, while I am caught up in external tumult, my sole thought, which continually belabors my soul with red-hot fear, is this: Your sole and highest goal has vanished. . . . I have tried to force myself to work, but I abhor all that bears the name of knowledge."

This letter was written in 1801, but Kleist never did solve for himself the problem he raised here. It is therefore relevant to the dramas and Novellen he wrote later. One might point to a parallel to his broodings about knowledge in his *Amphitryon*, where the very foundations of three lives are shaken by the problem of identity. What is identity, after all, but the knowledge of self? In connection with *Amphitryon*, we might also point to another problem, one which Kleist posed to his fiancée as an essay subject at about this time: who suffers more severely, the wife whose husband dies or the husband whose wife dies? Kleist's solution, arrived at through painfully tortuous reasoning, is that the husband suffers more. Again, we may point to a parallel of problem-posing in Jupiter-Amphitryon's question to Alkmene:

if Amphitryon, rather than the god, were to appear to you now, how would you feel about him and me?

In his restless state, Kleist decided to take a leave in 1801, went on a trip to Paris and then settled in Switzerland for a while. On the eve of his departure he wrote to his fiancée: "I am taking leave of you!—It seems to me as though it were forever. Like a child at play, I have ventured out to the middle of the sea; violent winds arise; the craft rocks dangerously in the waves; the rush of the sea deafens all reflection. I don't even know the direction in which I should steer, and a presentiment whispers to me that I am about to perish."

His waverings and uncertainties continue, moreover. In 1802, he writes to his sister that he would be ready to die after he had fulfilled three creative longings; he wants to sire a child, write a beautiful poem, and do a great deed. And yet, three weeks after wishing to sire a child, he writes to the long-suffering Wilhelmine that he will never return to Germany and breaks the engagement on the grounds that she is not strong enough to live as a peasant with him in Switzerland. His letter ends with the request that she never write him again.

In Switzerland, Kleist began his first drama, but he soon returned to Paris where he is supposed to have made a plan to assassinate Napoleon. After the plan failed, he had a breakdown and was hospitalized for five months. In 1804 he returned to Berlin, where he learned that there was no government position for him. Once again he started to write, first *The Broken Jug*, a comedy; then he started on *Amphitryon*, which began as a translation of Molière's drama. He also wrote *Penthesilea*, a highly emotional tragedy. With Adam Müller, he founded the periodical, *Phöbus*, and wrote to Goethe in an attempt to win the Olympian's support and, if possible, a contribution for the journal. Goethe, however, did not understand Kleist and had little sympathy for the young "hypochondriac," as he termed Kleist in 1809. In showing Kleist's *Jug* at the Weimar theater, Goethe had made the unpardonable error of cutting it into acts, which ruined a one-act play of over twenty scenes the effectiveness of which depends largely on rapid, uninterrupted presentation. He did not see much in *Penthesilea* to recommend it and refused his assistance to *Phöbus*. Goethe's remarks on *Amphitryon* will be quoted subsequently.

Kleist's last venture was a newspaper, *Berliner Abendblätter*, to which he contributed anecdotes, some essays and anti-Napoleonic writings. He had various difficulties with the authorities on this account.

Neither as a writer nor as a human being could Kleist successfully execute his plan for his life. His writings were not sufficiently appreciated during his life time to offer him compensation for his many frustrations. In 1810 Kleist met Henriette Vogel, a married woman who was incurably ill, presumably of cancer. Kleist's admiration of her soon turned to an adoration which lacked all rationality and all bounds. In 1811 they entered upon a suicide pact, and, after Kleist shot her, he killed himself.

Although Kleist lived for only thirty-four years, he is one of the outstanding German poets; his chief works are dramas and Novellen. Best known among the dramas are the above mentioned and *Kätchen from Heilbronn*, a fairytale drama; *The Hermann Battle*, which deals with the battle against the Romans in 9 A.D. but is fiercely patriotic and anti-French; and *The Prince of Homburg*, probably his most successful work. Among his Novellen *Michael Kohlhaas* is best known. As a writer, Kleist is a contemporary of the German Romantics and of Goethe. But aside from certain elements that reveal his time, Kleist stands alone, and his writings are characteristic only of himself.

II

As an introduction to Kleist's treatment of the Amphitryon material, only two previous Amphitryon dramas need be mentioned, the comedies of the Roman Plautus and of Molière.

The work of Plautus, dated in the third century B.C., is a typical Plautine comedy and has been tersely summed up by an acrostic of the first century B.C.:

Amore captus Alcumenae Juppiter
Mutavit sese in formam eius coniugis,
Pro patria Amphitruo dum decernit cum hostibus.

Habitu Mercurius ei subservit Sosiae.
Is advenientis servum ac dominum frustra habet.
Turbas uxori ciet Amphitruo, atque invicem
Raptant pro moechis. Blepharo captus arbiter
Uter sit non quit Amphitruo decernere.
Omnem rem noscunt. geminos Alcumena enititur![1]

Plautus dwells chiefly on the ridiculous elements of the situation which his narrator, Mercury, continually points out. Alcumena has very little to say and the birth of her twins has taken place off-stage when we hear about it. The twins are a miraculous pair: they have different fathers and were conceived three months apart! Amphitryon's son is a ten months' baby; Jupiter's, a seven months' child. In the narration concerning the birth of these twins, the feats of baby Hercules are also recounted.

A more satisfactory comedy by modern standards is Molière's *Amphitryon.* He begins with a satiric prologue in the course of which Night is persuaded to give Jupiter more time for his sport with Alcmène. The presentation that follows is light, and there is no opportunity to take any character seriously enough to instill doubts in the reader about the comic nature of the play. Molière has expanded the Sosias scenes and has cut out the narrative of Alcmène's delivery. Alcmène is rarely on stage and is given no opportunity to react to the news that Jupiter has given her a son who is to become a great hero. Molière thus has no complications arising out of hidden or patent implications which might imperil the comic nature of his play. To be sure, Sosias does comment rather dryly at the end and concludes the play with these words:

Tout cela va le mieux du monde,

---

[1] Jupiter, seized with love for Alcumena, changed his form to that of her husband, Amphitryon, while he was doing battle with the enemies for his country. Mercury, in the guise of Sosias, acted as his servant. On the return of the master and servant he dupes them. Amphitryon stirs up a storm with his wife, and in turn they charge adultery. Blepharo is made arbiter but cannot decide which is Amphitryon. (Then) all things are (made) known to them. Alcumena gives birth to twins.

Mais enfin coupons aux discours:
Et que chacun chez soi doucement se retire.
Sur telles affaires toujours
Le meilleur est de ne rien dire.

The tone of the whole has been such, however, that there is no need to infer tragic undertones from this statement.

Although Kleist called his *Amphitryon* (1807) a comedy, based on Molière's, his subtitle may be mainly interpreted as an acknowledgment of the source of most of the comic scenes. It is true that there are many comic elements, but the play could more properly be called a tragedy with comic scenes.

Goethe, who never did appreciate Kleist's work, which he did not even claim to understand very well, stated that he saw in the content of Kleist's *Amphitryon* nothing less than a translation of the Hercules myth into Christian terms! He pointed to the overshadowing of Mary by the Holy Ghost and compared it to Jupiter's visit to Alkmene. This, Goethe continued, is why the true Amphitryon has to be reconciled to the invasion of his private life and has to be made to consider it an honor. Were it not for this, he concluded, the situation of Alkmene would be painful, and Amphitryon would be in a cruel position indeed.

In the dialogue in which Jupiter suggests to Alkmene that a god spent the previous night with her and also in the announcement to Amphitryon that Alkmene is to bear a son, there are phrases which remind the reader of the relevant passages in the Bible. It seems, however, that the language used covers a similar situation rather than gives religious connotations. It certainly seems sacrilegious to compare the motivation of Jupiter, coming down to earth to have sport with mortal beauties, even if he did feel lonely on Olympus, with that of the Holy Ghost. The Christian comparison also fails because Alkmene, as Kleist has presented her, is no Mary, even though she does call herself an unworthy sinner! Goethe's alternative to the Christian equation has more merit. Kleist's "comedy" is indeed painful and cruel, and, were it not for the comic scenes, uncomfortable for the spectator or reader.

Even the character of Sosias is not devoid of tragedy. Sosias is obviously a traditional comic figure, the slave of Roman comedy, here promoted to servant standing. He is a loudmouthed coward, who often gets away with bold statements to his master but beats a hasty retreat as soon as the possibility of a beating is mentioned. His entering speech is full of his cowardice and his illusions of self-importance; his simple desire to escape beatings and to appease his growling stomach, growling all the more after the mention of sausages and cabbage, evokes a smile from even the sternest of mortals. But Sosias is also a tragic figure. Limited as he is in mental ability, he has nothing left to reassure him, once the one fact of his existence, as he grasps it, is pulled out from under him. If Mercury says that he is Sosias, looks and acts like him, and knows everything that Sosias did when he was alone, then Mercury must be Sosias, and Amphitryon's servant has lost his identity and, with it, his reason for living. The character of Sosias is drawn with a light hand, however, so that the tragic is still subordinated to his comic effect.

Amphitryon himself is a more traditional tragic hero, although his tragic high point is short-lived and vitiated by the denouement of the play. Amphitryon is presented from several points of view. First, we hear Sosias' rehearsal of his account to Alkmene in which Amphitryon is described with all the heroic conventions. Then we see Alkmene with Jupiter, whom she takes for Amphitryon, and find, next to the perfect admiration and love she has for her beloved husband, the undercurrent of Jupiter's criticism of the vain mortal who married Alkmene to found a great dynasty, who is vain about his military accomplishments, and takes Alkmene's love as a matter of course. Jupiter's presentation is necessarily colored by his jealous attempt to force Alkmene to discriminate between Amphitryon, her husband, and Jupiter, her lover. Amphitryon with Sosias or when reproaching Alkmene, however, does resemble Jupiter's assessment of him. When Amphitryon decides that Alkmene is incapable of lying and must therefore be mentally ill, he is still consistent with the vain mortal Jupiter made him out to be; this is also the case when the outraged Amphitryon confronts Jupiter and instructs his friends.

But Amphitryon assumes a

the impossible choice of calling

and more passionately as his fear of

adulteress and liar or of renouncing his o

and title, and his claim on her. As she stands

Amphitryon proclaims with great dignity for all t

hear that he would swear to the gods and stake his life

oath that Jupiter *is* indeed Amphitryon to Alkmene. Therefo

he proclaims, she is innocent of any moral or social transgres-
sion. In this speech he rises to heights of altruistic love which
are worthy of a tragic hero. He cannot maintain this height,
however, for Kleist follows the conventional plot and twists
Amphitryon back into it. Amphitryon reverts into a comic
character of sorts when he demands from the god Jupiter that
he be granted a divine son as compensation for sharing his wife
with the god. This expressed desire for vicarious satisfaction
brings Amphitryon back to the vainly practical mortal whom
Jupiter described to Alkmene as her husband.

Alkmene, however, is a perfect tragic heroine from her first to
her final appearance. We learn through the exposition that she is
an innocent child bride, very much in love with her husband
and so newly married that she can hardly believe that so much
pleasure as this union gives her can be legal fulfillment of
wifely duty. She delights in Amphitryon, his prowess, his im-
portance, his fame, his tenderness. During her daily prayers to
Jupiter, she endows the god, to whom she offers fervent prayers
for the well-being of her husband, with the facial features of
Amphitryon. She is surprised when Jupiter, to her Amphitryon,
her husband *and* lover, begins to distinguish between these two.
She cannot really follow him, nor does she want to do so.
She is so sure of her love and its wholesomeness that she wants
nothing problematic to mar its perfection. Jupiter, on the other
hand, who has already had to make a concession to her innocent
adoration of her husband by coming to her as Amphitryon,
convinces her with great difficulty that she should try to discriminate between husband and lover. Not at all convinced really,
but very much in love, she assures the dear man, who is *both*

. She really
 much under
 together and
ave lasted seven-

embarrassed to see
owered him with the
has given him all she
what hurt at his lack of
to him the events of the
ng, moreover, that she has
d, she is deeply hurt when
ity. She is too simple a woman
a   to do very well at hurling angry
reproa   thinks that he has found another
woman an   an excuse to leave his wife, but
when she is alo   aken in her self-assured innocence.
Brooding about the q   and looking closely at her sole proof
of innocence, the diadem of Labdacus, she suddenly discovers
the "J" inscribed on it. For the first time in her life, she is
unsure of herself. Could she, unwittingly, have wronged her
dear love after all?

Her conversation with Jupiter restores her inner harmony,
however. Jupiter is still Amphitryon to her when he convinces
her that she is incapable of wronging her love. He is most per-
suasive, for, as we know, he is the same wonderful lover who
gave her the most blissful night she has ever spent, and he
succeeds in making Amphitryon's peace with her, by declaring
that *he* is in her debt for any love she may have given the
impostor and by finally suggesting that the latter was none other
than Jupiter. Alkmene is so innocent that she cannot grasp the
whole fact of Jupiter's coming to *her* and finally states that
this was just a generous explanation, invented by Amphitryon to
cheer her. Jupiter, however, points to the initial on the diadem
as his proof.

At the insistent plea of Jupiter, who has tried to arouse her
sympathy with his presentation of the lonely, loveless Jovian

existence, Alkmene, back to her old self, promises that she will think about Jupiter one hour a day from now on, but that the rest of the day and the night will be given to thought of Amphitryon. But even the hour devoted to Jupiter is qualified when she states naively that it will be easy to think about the god now that she knows exactly what he looks like and no longer has to superimpose Amphitryon's features on him! Not satisfied completely, Jupiter asks how Alkmene would react if the god were to appear now. Alkmene states that she would be terrified, of course. And now Jupiter compounds the complexity of the identity problem, still seeking some satisfaction for himself, and proposes a problem that reminds the reader of the problems Kleist liked to pose to Wilhelmine von Zenge. If Alkmene had been talking to Jupiter all this time and Amphitryon were to appear now, how would she react? There is no problem for Alkmene in this. She is totally sure that she is with her dear Amphitryon now and has no difficulty in stating that she would want Amphitryon, were he not with her now and suddenly appeared, to be the god, so that her love, with whom she is now speaking, could stay with her. More of a confession of love, more success for his mission, even Jupiter could not have demanded!

Alkmene, who was wretched in her doubts after her quarrel with Amphitryon, is now totally restored in the confidence in the infallibility of her love and may even rejoice in the fact of a divine impostor. Her next encounter with Amphitryon is therefore an even greater blow to her than the first one was. Totally secure once again, she has been dining with Jupiter, who is Amphitryon to her, and has learned from him that there is a mortal who claims that he is the real Amphitryon. This, if a fact, would rob her of the Amphitryon with whom she is dining. If the mortal is the impostor, moreover, then she is restored to the position of being shamed. Fear and uncertainty again seize her. She had been so happy to be with her dear Amphitryon who was proud, as she must be too, that a god had come to her! In this frame of mind she confronts Amphitryon. What a shock to compare this mere mortal even to her husband (Jupiter, of course), for he falls short in every respect of the

man she takes to be her husband! She is terribly shocked and
bitterly hurt and cannot believe that she could have let herself
be violated by this ignoble, bad imitation-Amphitryon. It is for
this reason that she abuses him so fiercely, rejects him, and,
having pronounced Jupiter the real Amphitryon, decides to die.

When Jupiter begins to explain the preceding events and asks
whether she really thinks that Amphitryon appeared to her,
she begs him to spare her this enlightenment, for she fears
eternal disillusionment. The thought that this creature is her
husband is now highly repugnant to her. Her swooning in Amphitryon's arms at the sight of Jupiter in his divine form is therefore not to be interpreted as reconciliation. It is significant
that she sighs at the end of the play.[2] This is not the blissful sigh
of happiness of a woman who has fulfilled herself in love and
is restored to her lover, but rather that of a woman who has lost
her blind love for her husband. It is the sigh of disappointment
and resignation to an every-day existence after one has experienced bliss. It is the sigh of a woman who will never again
attain the high degree of inner harmony which the bride Alkmene
had. Husband and lover can never be one and the same for her
again, for she will always think of Jupiter as her lover and of
Amphitryon as the husband whom she is legally obligated to
love. The love of the highest god is more tragically destructive
to Alkmene, whose inner harmony he destroyed, than to Semele,
whom he consumed with his fire. Alkmene's sigh is tragic and
the remainder of her life, with her son Hercules as a constant
reminder of her one night of bliss, can never be innocent,
harmoniously serene, and happy.

Can this play be considered a comedy after all? Read it, and
see.

---

[2] One must question the interpretation Thomas Mann offers in his
brilliant essay, *Amphitryon,* when he states that Alkmene's final
sigh is the expression of a combination of the sweet confusion of
a woman's heart and a poet's dream. The confusion, if any
remains, is certainly bitter rather than sweet!

AMPHITRYON

CHARACTERS

JUPITER, identical in appearance to Amphitryon
MERCURY, identical in appearance to Sosias
AMPHITRYON, commander-in-chief of Thebes
SOSIAS, his servant
ALKMENE, Amphitryon's wife
CHARIS, Sosias' wife
The Generals
The Officers
Thebans

The action takes place in Thebes in front of the palace of
    Amphitryon.

ACT I

SCENE 1. *It is night.*

Sosias appears with a lantern.

Sosias: Hey there! Who's that sneak over there? Ho there! If only
Day would break, I'd be so glad; the night is—how's that?
I am your friend, good folk! We share the same road—
This fellow you've just met, me,—I'm most honest,
I promise you, most honest of all men under the sun—
Or at the moment I should say, under the moon's light—
They're either rascals, scoundrels who lack courage,
Afraid of making an attack on me, or else
The wind was rustling through the leaves.
A sound of any kind howls in these mountains.   10
Careful now! Slowly! But if my hat
Does not soon touch the Theban town
I want to go to darkest Orcus.
Oh, hang it all! My lord and master
Could well have tested in another way
My courage and my faithful disposition.
The whole world crowns his head with fame and honor
But sending me away long after midnight
Is really just a trick of meanness.
Some love of fellow man and some consideration   20
I should esteem as highly as I do
The wedge of virtue he employs
To scatter hostile hosts.
"Good servant Sosias," he said, "prepare at once
To go to Thebes; there tell about my vict'ry,

3

And then inform my loving lady
That I shall soon get home."
But, if that couldn't wait until tomorrow,
I'll be a horse, with saddle, if you like!
But look! I think I see our house!   30
Great guns! You've made it, Sosias!
May pardon come to all your enemies!
Now friend, think carefully about your mission;
With pomp they'll lead you to the lady's presence.
There'll be Alkmene whom you then must give
Complete report, with rhetor's skill,
About Amphitryon's encounter with the enemy
In which he won the vict'ry for his land.
—But, devil take it all, how shall I do that?
I wasn't even there! Oh damn it all, I wish   40
I'd looked out of the tent from time to time
When the two armies battled hand to hand.
Oh well!—I guess, if I just talk of shots and beatings,
I'll manage just as well as others do
Who've never heard a whistling arrow either.—
A little dress rehearsal might not be amiss!
Right smart, my lad! Try yourself out.
Let's say: the audience room is here, and this
Old lantern is Alkmene, my lady, on her throne.

(*He sets the lantern down.*)

Most noble lady!—Amphitryon dispatched me,   50
My lofty lord and your most noble husband,
To bring to you the happy news
Of his great vict'ry over the Athenians.
—A fine start this!—"Ah, truly dearest Sosias
I shall not moderate my joy
At seeing you again."—This kindness,
Exalted lady, shames me, modest as I am,
Although your words would fill another man with pride.
—You see—that isn't so bad either—"And how

Does fare my soul's dear love, how is   60
Amphitryon?"—Ah, gracious lady, I can sum that up:
Just like a man of heart upon a field of glory!
—Ah, hot stuff! Watch that line!—"When will he come then?"
Surely no later than his work permits,
Though not as soon perhaps as he would wish.
—Great stuff!—"And did he tell you nothing else
To say to me dear Sosias?"—He says but little
Rather acts, and all the world does tremble
At the mention of his name.
—Well, I'll be damned! Since when am I so witty?—   70
"You say then the Athenians are withdrawing?"
—They are; and Labdacus, their leader is now dead;
Pharissa has been stormed and won and all the mountains
Resound with echoing cries of victory.—
"Oh, dearest Sosias! Look, you must tell me
All that elaborately, sparing no detail."
—I'm at your service, gracious lady.
Indeed, I dare say, I can give
Complete detail about this victory:
If you would be so kind, imagine now   80
Right here—(*He designates the places on his hand.*) Pharissa
—which is a city, as you surely know,
As large in size, roughly,
Lest I exaggerate, if not a trifle larger
Than Thebes! Here flows the river. Our men
In battle order on a hillside here.
And down there in the valley—
The enemy in countless numbers
Now after sending up an oath to heaven
So that the clouds did tremble all about,   90
He thrusts himself, his orders sharply given,
With floods upon us, roaring all the while.
No less courageous 'though, we showed
Him the way back—and you will soon see how.
First he encountered the advance troops—here—

Which then withdrew—then he met the archers—over there—
Then they withdrew. Made bold now, he attacks
The catapulters; they then cleared his way.
And when he boldly did approach the main corps,
It hurled—no, stop!—That's not quite right about the main
corps.   100
—I hear a noise from over there, I think.

SCENE 2

Mercury leaves Amphitryon's house as Sosias.

MERCURY (*to himself*): If this uncalled-for rascal over there
Is not removed from here in time by me,
By river Styx, the bliss stands in the balance
Which Zeus is seeking in Alkmene's arms
Which to enjoy today th'Olympian,
Appearing as Amphitryon, descended to this earth.
SOSIAS (*without seeing Mercury*): 'Tis nothing to be sure; my
fear is vanishing,
But to elude th'adventurers
I want to get home all the way   110
And free myself of my commission.
MERCURY (*to himself*): You'll have to conquer Mercury, my
friend,
Or how to keep you from it, I shall know.
SOSIAS: But this night is of truly endless length.
If I've not been five hours on my way,
Five hours measured by the Theban sun disk,
Then I shall shoot it off the tower piece by piece.
Either the drunkenness of victory
Has made my master view the evening as morning
Or unrestrainéd Phoebus is still sleeping,   120
Because he drank too much last night.
MERCURY: How disrespectfully that rascal over there

Speaks of the gods. A little patience;
This arm of mine will soon teach him respect.
SOSIAS (*sees Mercury*): Ah, by the gods of night! I'm lost.
A thief prowls 'round the house whom I
Shall soon or later at the gallows see.
I must pretend I'm cheeky, brazen, confident. (*He whistles.*)
MERCURY (*aloud*): Who is that lout there,
Assuming for himself such liberties   130
As though he were at home here—
To din perpetually in my ears with whistling?
Perhaps the dancing of my stick should keep him company?
SOSIAS: He does not seem to be a friend of music.
MERCURY: I haven't found a soul since last week
Whose bones I could have broken.
My arm is getting stiff, I feel, with all this rest,
And what I'm seeking is a back as wide as yours
To get back into practice.
SOSIAS: Who, devil take him, gave this fellow life?   140
I'm seized by deadly terrors, I can feel it,
Which cause my breath to stop.
Had he been spewn out by the jaws of hell,
More terror could his sight not hold for me.
—Howe'er, perhaps that fool feels just like me,
And now he only tries the bully's part
T'intimidate me, scare me stiff.
Stop chap, for I can do that too. And by the by,
I am alone; so's he; I have two fists,
He has no more, and should my luck desert me,   150
I can retreat in safety over there. So forward march!
MERCURY (*gets in his way*): Halt! Who goes there?
SOSIAS: I do.
MERCURY: Which I is that?
SOSIAS: Mine, if you please. And mine, I think
Walks here in safety, just like others. Courage, Sosias!
MERCURY: Stop! You won't escape with such light reckoning.
What's your position?

SOSIAS: What's my position?
  Why, one on two feet, as you see.
MERCURY: I want to know: are you a lord or servant?
SOSIAS: After you've looked at me both this and that way
  Am I a lord, am I a servant?   160
MERCURY: It's settled. I dislike you.
SOSIAS: Dear me, I'm sorry.
MERCURY: In short, you traitor, I just want to know,
  Unworthy alley-walker, loiterer
  Who you may be, where from and where you're going,
  And how you come to loiter here.
SOSIAS: I cannot answer anything to that
  But this—I am a human being, come from there,
  Go this way, and have ought ahead
  Which now begins to make time very long for me.
MERCURY: I see you're witty, and you've gotten started   170
  In making short your riddance of me. But I begin
  To feel like making longer our acquaintance,
  T'initiate the involvement, I shall now
  Hit you behind the ear with this my hand.
SOSIAS: Me?
MERCURY: You; and now you can be sure of it.
  What will be your decision now?
SOSIAS: By Jove,
  You hit with a strong hand, my friend.
MERCURY: That was a medium one. At times I hit
  Still better.
SOSIAS: Were I in such a mood
  We'd really have a fight.   180
MERCURY: That would be fine with me. I love such dealings.
SOSIAS: But on account of bus'ness, I must take my leave. (*about
  to go*)
MERCURY (*blocks his way*): Whereto?
SOSIAS: Oh hell, what business of yours?
MERCURY: I want to know
  I tell you, where you're going.

SOSIAS: That is the gate
 Which I want opened for me. Let me go.
MERCURY: If you have the audacity
 T'approach that palace gate, there will
 Beat down on you a storm of blows.
SOSIAS: Eh? I'm not to be allowed to enter home?
MERCURY: Home? Say that again.
SOSIAS: All right.   190
 Home's what I said.
MERCURY: You claim to be of this house?
SOSIAS: Why not? Is't not Amphitryon's house?
MERCURY: Is this Amphitryon's house? Of course,
 You rascal. It's Amphitryon's house,
 The palace of the leading Theban general,
 But what do you conclude?
SOSIAS: What's my conclusion?
 That I shall enter. I'm his servant.
MERCURY: His serv........?
SOSIAS: His servant.
MERCURY: You?
SOSIAS: Yes, me.
MERCURY: Amphitryon's servant?
SOSIAS: Amphitryon's servant, servant of Thebes' general.
MERCURY: —Your name is?
SOSIAS: Sosias.
MERCURY: So........?
SOSIAS: Sosias.   200
MERCURY: Now listen you. I'll break your every bone.
SOSIAS: Are you
 Insane?
MERCURY: Who, shameless one gave you the right
 To take Sosias' name?
SOSIAS: I do not take it; it was given me.
 Let my old man be held responsible.
MERCURY: Whoever heard of such audacity?
 Shameless, you dare to tell me to my face

That you're Sosias.

SOSIAS: Exactly.
And this for the just reason that
The great gods wish it so; because   210
I do not have the pow'r to fight against them,
To want to be another than I am;
Because I must be *Me*, Amphitryon's servant,
Although I'd ten times rather be Amphitryon,
Or else his cousin or his broth'r-in-law.

MERCURY: Just wait! I'll try to work your transformation.

SOSIAS: Oh citizens! Oh Thebans! Murderers! Thieves!

MERCURY: You, worthless creature, dare to scream?

SOSIAS: How's that?
You beat me and I may not cry for help?

MERCURY: It's night, don't you know that, and time to sleep   220
And don't you know that in this castle
Alkmene sleeps, Amphitryon's wife?

SOSIAS: Oh, go, be hanged!
I must accept defeat, because you see
I have no whip to use; you do.
But giving beatings without being beaten back
Is not heroic! I can tell you that!
It's bad, if one displays one's courage
Against a man who's forced by fate to hide his.

MERCURY: Let's get the facts then. Who are you?

SOSIAS (*to himself*):   If I
Escape that one, I'll pour on earth   230
As off'ring half a flask of wine.

MERCURY: You claim to be Sosias still?

SOSIAS: Oh, let me go.
Your stick can work it, so I'll be no longer,
Not that I won't be me, since I am that.
The only diff'rence is that now I feel
Myself to be Sosias who's been beaten.

MERCURY: Watch out, you cur! I'll cool you off! (*makes
    threatening gesture*):

SOSIAS: Don't, don't.
  Stop your attack on me.
MERCURY: Not 'til
  You stop—
SOSIAS: All right. I'll stop.
  No word I'll counter, you'll be right.   240
  Whate'er you'll say, I shall agree.
MERCURY: Are you still Sosias then, you treacherous lout?
SOSIAS: Alas!
  I now am what you will. Command what I
  Shall be. Your stick makes you the master of my life.
MERCURY: You said you'd called yourself Sosias other times?
SOSIAS: It's true. I'd wrongly thought until this very moment
  That this was right.
  But now the weight of your strong reasons
  Has taught me, and I now see my mistake.
MERCURY: I am the one who calls himself Sosias.
SOSIAS: Sosias........? 250
  You........?
MERCURY: Indeed. Sosias. And anyone who wants to fool
    around
  Is to beware of this my stick.
SOSIAS (to himself): Y'eternal gods! So I must
  Renounce myself now, let my name
  Be stolen by a liar?
MERCURY: I hear you murmur in your teeth.
SOSIAS: Nothing that really would offend you.
  But by the gods of all of Greece
  Do I beseech you now, the gods who rule us both,
  Give me permission for a moment   260
  To speak with you quite candidly.
MERCURY: Speak then.
SOSIAS: But will your stick now play a silent role?
  Not enter into conversation? Promise me
  We'll have an armistice.
MERCURY: All right, so let it be.

I'll grant this point.

SOSIAS: Well, now tell me
How does this mad idea come to you
Of shamelessly absconding with my name?
Were it my coat, or were't my supper,
I'd understand. But why a name? Can you now wear it?
Or eat it? Drink it perhaps? Or even pawn it?   270
What good is such a theft to you?

MERCURY: How's that? You—you'd dare?

SOSIAS: Stop! Stop! I say
We have a truce.

MERCURY: You shameless one!
Completely worthless!

SOSIAS: I'm not opposed to that.
Abusive words I like. With those
One can continue to converse.

MERCURY: You call yourself Sosias?

SOSIAS: Yes, I admit it. An unsubstantiated rumor
Has given me—

MERCURY: Enough. The truce is ended
And I'll take up my word again.

SOSIAS: Oh, go to hell! I can't destroy myself,   280
Nor work a transformation. Nor can I shed my skin
And drape it then about your shoulders.
Has ever man experienced such since time began?
Is this a dream perhaps? Did I take too much morning sustenance?
Am I not fully conscious?
Did not Amphitryon send me here
To tell the lady he's returning?
Shall I not tell her of the victory he won
And how Pharissa has surrendered?
Do I not hold this lantern? Did I not find   290
You, loit'ring at this very door?
And when I wanted to approach the gate
Did you not take the stick and beat

My back inhumanly til it was black and blue?
Insisting to my face that it's not me
But rather you that serves Amphitryon, my lord?
I feel that this is, sadly, but too true;
Would that it pleased the gods that I were mad!

MERCURY: Careful, you rascal, for my rage will in another minute
Rain down on you like hail stones once again!   300
What you have said, each word, each single one
Is true of me: except the beating.

SOSIAS: Of you?—The lantern here is, by the gods,
My witness—

MERCURY: You lie, I say, you traitor and deceiver
Amphitryon has sent me here.
To me the Theban general gave only yesterday,
Still covered with the dust of murd'rous battle,
Leaving the temple where he'd sacrificed to Mars,
The proper orders to report his victory in Thebes
And that the hostile general,   310
Named Labdacus, had fallen by his hand.
For I am Sosias, I'll tell you that,
His servant, son of Davus, that good shepherd,
Who, born right here, brother of Harpagon,
Did die on foreign soil: my wife is Charis
Whose moods enrage me;
I then am Sosias; I sat in the little tower.
And on my backside did they lately count off fifty blows
Because I'd carried honesty too far.

SOSIAS (to himself): He's right in this. And if one's not   320
Sosias oneself one cannot be informed
Of all the things he seems to know.
Indeed, one must believe him just a little bit.
Besides, now that I see him closely,
His looks, his height, his manner are all mine,
He even has my rascal-like expression.
—I must ask him a few more questions
To straighten out myself. (Aloud) Say, tell me

About the booty from the hostile camp,
How did Amphitryon plan its distribution   330
And what did he desire to be his share?
MERCURY: He took the diadem of Labdacus,
    Found in the latter's tent.
SOSIAS: And what was then done to this diadem?
MERCURY: Amphitryon's initial was engraved,
    Gleaming, upon its golden brow.
SOSIAS (*to himself*): He wears it now—?
MERCURY: Alkmene
    Is to have it. She will wear the jewel
    As vict'ry's souvenir around her waist.
SOSIAS: This present will be sent her   340
    From the camp—?
MERCURY: In a gilt box on which
    Amphitryon has put his coat of arms.
SOSIAS (*to himself*): He knows it all! By all the devils then!
    In earnest I begin to doubt myself.
    His shamelessness and stick already
    Have made him Sosias. This now was all I needed!
    He makes himself be Sosias for good reasons.
    'Though when I touch myself, I still could swear:
    My body is all Sosias!
    —How can I find my way out of this labyrinth?   350
    The things I did when I was all alone,
    The things that no one saw, no one can know
    Unless he's really me, just as I am.
    —All right, this is the question then to cast some light.
    Why not? This now will catch him—well, we'll see now.
    (*aloud*): When both the armies fought in closest combat
    What did you do, tell me, there by the tents,
    Where cleverly you'd found a way to sneak?
MERCURY: Well, from a ham—
SOSIAS (*to himself*):   The devil's got this fellow—
MERCURY: Which I found in a corner of the tent   360
    I cut myself a juicy center slice

And then adroitly opened up a wineskin
To put myself into a cheerful mood
Against the battle being fought outside.
SOSIAS (*to himself*): It's over now! It would not even matter now
    If earth were to consume me on the spot,
    For from this wineskin one can only drink
    If one by chance finds, as I did,
    The key that fits right in it.
    (*aloud*): I now see, my old friend, you really are   370
    Th'entire serving of a Sosias for which
    There's use upon this earth.
    It seems superfluous to carry on.
    Far be't from me to play th'aggressive one,
    And gladly do I cede to you. Only
    Have now the kindness please to tell me,
    Since I'm not Sosias, who I am.
    For something, you'll admit, I have to be.
MERCURY: When Sosias I shall no longer be,
    You may be he, that is all right, I'm willing.   380
    But now, as long as I am he, you'll risk your neck,
    If you should get the brazen notion.
SOSIAS: All right, all right, my head begins to whirl.
    Indeed I now see how things stand,
    Although I can't yet grasp it all the way.
    Howe'er—this matter must come to an end now,
    And the most clever way to make it end
    Is that I leave.—Farewell! (*approaches the house*).
MERCURY (*pushing him back*): How's that again, you hangman's
    bait! Must I
    Lame all your bones? (*He hits Sosias.*)
SOSIAS: Oh ye just gods!   390
    Where's your protection now? My back
    Won't heal for weeks, e'en if Amphitryon
    Does not beat me again. All right. I'll now avoid
    That devil there and go back to the camp.
    Though darkly leers at me this hellish night.—

This was a mission bringing me great honor!
How will your master greet you, Sosias? (*Off.*)

SCENE 3

MERCURY: Well, gone at last! You should have left before.
You would have spared yourself some cuts and bruises.—
That rascal doesn't realize how greatly he was honored;   400
Not every man gets beatings from a god!
I must admit, I did it like the best of jailers.
Well, be that as it may. He's sinned enough,
Though not today, to merit such a beating.
He'll have it on account.—
I only hope, with all his screaming—
Roasted alive, he could have screamed no louder—
He did not wake the lovers.—By my immortal life,
Lord Zeus is leaving. The father of the gods appears
And tenderly Alkmene walks with him   410
As though he were her dear Amphitryon.

SCENE 4

Jupiter as Amphitryon, Alkmene, Charis, Mercury. Torches.

JUPITER: Alkmene, dearest love, have them remove
The torches over there. 'Tis true, their light
Shines on the sweetest loveliness which blooms on earth
And no Olympian ever saw more beauty;
And yet—how shall I say it? They also do reveal
The one who has been lured here by your charm, beloved.
It would be better, it remained a secret
That your Amphitryon was here in Thebes.
I've snatched these moments from the war   420

To bring them as a sacrifice to love.
The world might misinterpret such a theft;
I should be glad to have no witness of it
Other than just the one who reaped its benefits.
ALKMENE: Amphitryon! You want to leave me now? How
    burdensome
Is fame like yours, beloved.
How gladly would I trade the diadem,
You won for me in battle, for just
A little bunch of violets
Picked all around a lowly hut.   430
We only need each other. Why then
Is so much alien matter forced upon you,
Baton and crown, the symbols of your office?
'Tis true, whene'er the populace rejoices in you
And spends its rapture in each of your great names,
It does make sweet the thought that you belong to me;
But can such brief delight begin to compensate
For all the fear I feel when in the battle,
An arrow aims to wound you, dearest heart?
How empty does this house become without you!   440
How slothfully the cheerful dance of hours proceeds
To bring me day, when you are gone!
Alas, the deprivation I must suffer for my country
I've only come to realize today, Amphitryon,
When you were all my own for two brief hours.
JUPITER: My love! What rapture you provoke! But still
You also rouse one care in me, which I,
As trivial as it sounds, must bring before you.
You know there is a matrimonial law,
A duty too, and that the man who is deprived of love   450
Can stand before a judge t'demand his due.
The fact that such a law exists disturbs
My greatest happiness, for I should like,
My dearest one, to thank your heart
For every grace you grant me. I don't like

To think that you're complying with a legal form
Which you imagine binding.
How easily you could dispel this tiny doubt!
I beg you then: reveal yourself completely
And tell me now, did you receive your legal spouse   460
This day or did you greet your lover?

ALKMENE: Belovéd, husband! What does all this mean?
Am I not solely justified in loving you this way
By this, the sacredness of our relationship?
How can the world's law torture you,
A law that not at all restrains in this
But rather tears away most fortunately
Whatever barriers stand between most daring wishes
And all the joy of their fulfillment.

JUPITER: My feeling for you, dearest love,   470
Surpasses far, by solar distance
What I owe you as husband. Forget, I beg,
My love, the husband now; discriminate
Between myself and him, because disgraceful
Is confusion of this sort and painful to me.
I simply cannot bear the thought at all
That you have just received the idiot
Who coldly deems himself to have a claim on you.
My wish, sweet light, is that I did appear
To you as a distinctly separate person.   480
I conquered you, because the great gods did
Themselves teach me the art of winning you.
Why then confuse me with the Theban general,
That vain Amphitryon, who courted recently
A wealthy prince's daughter for a great house?
What do you say to that? You see, I want to leave
Your virtue all intact for him, that public fool,
And keep your love reserved for me alone.

ALKMENE: Amphitryon! You're jesting. If people here
Heard you say all these scornful things about Amphitryon,   490
They'd have to think that you were someone else,

I don't know who. They'd never think I'd merely let it slip
This cheerful night that oftentimes the lover can outdo the
    husband.
But since the gods united both in you for me
I gladly do forgive the lover
Where the husband did perhaps fall short.
JUPITER: Then promise me that you will not forget
This happy feast of being reunited:
That this divine day which we lived together,
My dearest love, you never will confuse   500
With common ev'ryday occurrences of married life.
Promise, I say, that you will think of me
When at some future time Amphitryon returns—?
ALKMENE: If you insist, what can I say?
JUPITER: I thank you!
This means more than you think!
Farewell; my duty calls.
ALKMENE: You'd leave me?
Not give, dear love, perfection to our brief night
Which flees us rapidly on countless wings?
JUPITER: Did you find this night shorter than the others?
ALKMENE: Oh!
JUPITER: Sweet child! Aurora could do no more   510
For our joint bliss than she has done.
Farewell. I'll see to it that all the other nights
Take no more time than earth demands of them.
ALKMENE: I think he is intoxicated. So am I. (*Off.*)

SCENE 5

Mercury. Charis.

CHARIS (*to herself*): That's tenderness all right. That's real
    fidelity!
A proper celebration for a couple,

After long separation reunited!
That peasant over there who's wed to me,
He is another sort—as tender as a brick.
MERCURY (*to himself*): Now I must hasten to arouse the night 520
Lest our world's orb lose all its order.
The good matchmaking goddess now has tarried
Seventeen hours for us here in Thebes;
Now she may wander on so she may hide
With her veil more adventures.
CHARIS (*aloud*): There goes that creature without warmth or
   feeling.
MERCURY: Should I not follow lord Amphitryon?
If he goes off to camp, should I
Just idly loiter here?
CHARIS: You could say something.
MERCURY: Something indeed. There's
   time for that   530
I've answered all your questions. That suffices.
In this respect I'm quite laconic.
CHARIS: A clod, is what you are. Dear wife, one says,
Keep loving me, cheer up, and so on.
MERCURY: Oh, damn it all! What are you thinking of? Should I,
To while away the time, sit with you making faces?
Eleven married years exhaust all talk;
I said it all to you eons ago.
CHARIS: Deceiver that you are, look at Amphitryon,
Showing his tenderness like simple folk,   540
And be ashamed that, in devotion to his wife
And in connubial love, a lord
Of the great world surpasses you.
MERCURY: He still is on his honeymoon, my child.
There is an age at which all things are proper.
What's proper to these two young lovers
I'd like to watch from a great distance
If we were doing it. We'd be a laughing stock
If two old asses such as we are

Would toss sweet nothings at each other.   550
CHARIS: You ruffian! What kind of talk is that?
   You think that I am capable no longer—?
MERCURY: I wouldn't say that.
   Your obvious damage can be overlooked,
   And in the dark, you're gray; but here,
   As on the open market place, there'd be a riot
   If hell gave me the notion to make passes at you.
CHARIS: You traitor. Did I not go, as soon as you appeared,
   To wash and comb my hair and change
   Into this clean, fresh dress.
   All that, to have you spurn and scorn me.   560
MERCURY: This clean fresh dress indeed! If you could take off
   first
   The dress that nature gave you, then I wouldn't mind
   That dirty apron you've got on.
CHARIS: When you were courting me you liked it well enough.
   That's when I should have put it on, there in the kitchen,
   While washing or while helping with the hay.
   Is it my fault that time has left its mark?
MERCURY: No, dearest wife. But I can't patch it either.
CHARIS: You, scoundrel, don't deserve to have
   A wife of good repute and honor.   570
MERCURY: I shouldn't mind, had you less honor
   If you would only stop the deafening din
   Of your eternal quarreling.
CHARIS: How's that? So you don't like that I
   Maintained my honor and a spotless reputation?
MERCURY: May heav'n preserve me! Cherish your virtue
   But it does not have to be a sleigh horse
   With tinkling bells in streets and market place.
CHARIS: You would deserve the kind of wife one finds in Thebes,
   A tricky rascal, full of wicked plots.   580
   One that would drown you with sweet words
   So you would swallow cuckoldry with them.
MERCURY: As far as that's concerned, I'll tell you frankly:

Imagined evils only torture fools.
And I am rather envious of the man
Who has a friend who lends connubial payment to him.
That man will then live on to ripe old age
And live the lives of all his children.

CHARIS: You have so little shame; you'd egg me on?
    You'd be so bold that you would urge   590
    That I should join you with the friendly Theban
    Who follows me at night?

MERCURY: Hell, yes. If you would only spare me then
    From listening to your account of it.
    I think a comfortable sin is worth as much
    As noisome virtue; and my motto is:
    A little less of honor here in Thebes and more tranquility.
    Farewell then, little treasure, Charis dear. I have to go.
    Amphitryon has probably reached camp already. (*Off.*)

CHARIS: Why do I now lack the decisive courage   600
    To punish with an obvious act
    My despicable husband. Oh, ye gods!
    How I regret it now, that all the world
    Considers me an honorable woman!

ACT II

SCENE 1. *It is day*.

Amphitryon. Sosias.

AMPHITRYON: Shut up, you thief and scoundrel, you
Confounded rascal. You good-for-nothing,
Don't you know that all this jabbering
Will bring you to the gallows?
And I just lack a heavy cane
To treat you properly according to my wrath.   610
SOSIAS: If that's your tone with me, I'll say no more.
I'll dream, or just be drunk, as you command.
AMPHITRYON: To think that you would tell me such a tale quite
    shamelessly!
A tale like those that nurses whisper
Into children's ears at eventide.—
D'you think I'd give such nonsense any credence?
SOSIAS: Indeed not! You are the master and I am your servant
And you will do exactly as you wish.
AMPHITRYON: So be it. I shall repress my anger,
Force myself to be patient long enough   620
To hear the whole account again from the beginning.
—I have to solve this dev'lish puzzle for myself,
Until I do I shan't set foot into that house.
—And now pull all your wits together, Sosias,
And give detailed accounting, word for word.
SOSIAS: Forgive me lord, but first, before I tell my tale,
I'm so afraid, lest I offend you, sire,

23

Please tell me what's the tone of this negotiation?
In speaking should I follow my convictions,
Being an honest man, you understand, or should I   630
Speak to you, sire, as is the wont at court?
Shall I just boldly speak the truth, or shall I
Demean myself as does befit a proper man at court?

AMPHITRYON: Stop all this nonsense. I demand of you
Immediate   complete   report.

SOSIAS: All right. Then let me do it. You shall be served.
You merely have to toss the questions to me.

AMPHITRYON: Having received your orders from me—?

SOSIAS: I took,
Going through hellish darkness, the road to Thebes.
It was as though the day had sunk ten thousand fathoms.   640
I cursed you and the mission thoroughly and went on to your
     palace.

AMPHITRYON: What's that you say, you rascal?

SOSIAS: It's the truth, my lord.

AMPHITRYON: All right. Go on then. As you were following the
     road—?

SOSIAS: I put each foot in turn ahead of me
And left the tracks that I had made behind me.

AMPHITRYON: What's this! I want to know what you en-
     countered!

SOSIAS: Nothing, my lord. But I can tell you that I
Was full of fear and horror, salva venia.

AMPHITRYON: When you arrived here—?

SOSIAS: I practiced just a little
The speech I was to make   650
And cleverly imagined that the lantern
Was your dear wife, the princess.

AMPHITRYON: This done—?

SOSIAS: I was disturbed. It's coming now.

AMPHITRYON: Disturbed? By what? Who interrupted you?

SOSIAS: Sosias.

AMPHITRYON: How am I to interpret this?

SOSIAS: How are you to in-
   terpret?
  I swear, you ask too much of me.
  Sosias did interrupt when I was practicing.
AMPHITRYON: Sosias! Which Sosias! What kind
  Of hangman's bait or scoundrel Sosias
  Who lives in Thebes and bears your name   660
  Would interrupt your practice of your speech?
SOSIAS: Sosias! He's your servant.
  You sent him from your camp but yesterday
  T'nnounce your coming to the palace.
AMPHITRYON: You? Eh?
SOSIAS: Yes! An I that has all knowledge
  Of all the secrets that we have.
  An I that knows about the box and diamonds
  An I, just like the I that's speaking with you now.
AMPHITRYON: What kind of tale is that!
SOSIAS: A true one.
  If I am lying, sire, may I die at once.   670
  Before me, had this I arrived upon the scene.
  And in this case, I had arrived, I swear,
  Before I got here.
AMPHITRYON: Where do you get this foolish chatter? This wishy-
  washy stuff?
  Is this a dream? Is it intoxication?
  Some madness on your part? Or could it be a jest?
SOSIAS: I'm absolutely serious, sire, and,
  Upon my word of honor, you will kindly
  Give me your credence. I swear to you
  That I, who singly left your camp,   680
  Doubly arrived in Thebes;
  I met me here with staring eyes.
  This I that's standing here before you now
  Is totally worn out with weariness and hunger.
  The other I came from your house,
  Was all refreshed, encountered there a devil of a fellow,

And both these scoundrels, jealous of each other,
Both of them eager to complete your mission,
Began to fight at once, and I,
I had to go back to the camp   690
Because I was a foolish rascal.
AMPHITRYON: One has to be as gentle as I am,
Peaceful and self-effacing, too,
To let a servant speak in such a way.
SOSIAS: My lord, if you're annoyed, I'll say no more.
Let's talk of something else.
AMPHITRYON: All right, go on. You see I'm calm.
I'll hear you patiently until the end.
But tell me, by your conscience now,
Is there a shade of probability   700
In anything you tell to me as truth?
Can one grasp, comprehend, make sense of it?
SOSIAS: Of course not. Who would demand that of you?
I'd send him to the madhouse who would claim
He understood ought of this whole affair.
It lacks all rhyme and reason,
A troll-like incident, just like a fairy-tale
And still as true as sunlight.
AMPHITRYON: If, in that case, one were to have five senses, how
could one believe it?
SOSIAS: Upon my soul! It cost me bitter pain   710
Just like yourself, before I learned to give it credence.
I thought myself possessed when at this place
I found my person stationed, making noise,
And for a long time cursed me for a scoundrel.
But in the end, I realized that I just had
To recognize myself, one I just like the other.
It stood, as though the air around me were a mirror,
Right here in front of me: a being, totally like me,
Having my bearing and my stature too.
Two drops of water are not more alike.   720
Yes, had it been more sociable,

Not such a moody ruffian, I might have
Been quite pleased with it, I swear.
AMPHITRYON: To how much continence I've been condemned!
But tell me at long last, did you not go into the house?
SOSIAS: Into the house! How's that! You are a fine one! How?
Would I permit it? Yield to good reason? Did I not
Stubbornly continue to refuse me entry?
AMPHITRYON: What? How? Oh hell!
SOSIAS: How? With a stick
Of which my back still shows the traces. 730
AMPHITRYON: So someone beat you?
SOSIAS: You're telling me!
AMPHITRYON: Who hit you then?
SOSIAS: I did.
AMPHITRYON: You hit yourself?
SOSIAS: Indeed I did! Not, to be sure, this I right here and now;
Th'accurséd I there, at the house,
The I that beats like five strong oarsmen.
AMPHITRYON: For speaking thus to me, may you have much mis-
fortune!
SOSIAS: If you would like to see it, sire, I can show you.
The witness whom you must believe
Was my companion in my suffering: my aching back.
—The I that chased me from here had 740
A strong advantage: it had courage
And arms just like a boxer.
AMPHITRYON: To end all this. You've spoken with my wife?
SOSIAS: No.
AMPHITRYON: Why didn't you?
SOSIAS: Well, for the best of reasons.
AMPHITRYON: And who made you neglect your duty?
You cur, deceiver, worthless one!
SOSIAS: Must I repeat it ten times ten times more?
I did, I told you that; this devil-I
Had taken full possession of the door;
It was that I that wants to be the sole one, 750

That I there at the house, wielding my stick,
The I that beat me half to death.

AMPHITRYON: The beastly creature must be drunk enough
To lose the little brain it had before.

SOSIAS: If I have had more than my share
Of drink today, then may the devil take me.
My oath, upon my soul, you can believe me!

AMPHITRYON: Well, did you overdo the sleeping?
Have you perhaps had nightmares
Which showed you these mad happenings   760
Which you tell me as honest truth—?

SOSIAS: No, nothing of the sort. I have not slept this day
And didn't feel like sleeping in the woods.
Awake, fully alert, I did arrive here;
And very much awake and lively was the other
Sosias, who gave to me the beating of my life.

AMPHITRYON: Be silent now. Why should I strain my brain?
I'm mad to listen to this wishy-washy nonsense.
This useless drivel, full of folly,
Is totally bereft of human brain and reason.   770
Follow me now.

SOSIAS (to himself): That's how it goes. Because I say it,
It's nonsense, not worth hearing.
But, had a great man flayed himself,
It would be called a miracle indeed.

AMPHITRYON: Tell them to open up the gate for me. Look!
There comes my wife, Alkmene. She'll be surprised now
Since she has not been told of my arrival.

SCENE 2

Alkmene. Charis. Amphitryon. Sosias.

ALKMENE: Come, Charis dear. Let's show the gods
Our gratitude by off'ring at their altar.

Let's pray that they will go on granting   780
Their sacred, powerful protection to the best of husbands.

(*She sees Amphitryon.*)

Oh God! Amphitryon.
AMPHITRYON: May heaven grant
That I don't frighten my belovéd wife!
Alkmene will not be less tender to me
After so short a separation, I do hope,
For I am still Amphitryon who has returned.
ALKMENE: You're back so soon—?
AMPHITRYON: How's that? This exclamation,
An ambiguous sign indeed it seems to be to me,
E'en though the gods fulfilled that wish of hers.
This "back so soon," by Jove, is not   790
The welcome of a burning passion.
I've been a fool; I had the grand delusion
That war had kept me far away too long;
As I had figured it, I'm coming late.
But you show my mistake to me quite clearly,
And with surprise I do perceive that I
Snow in on you unneeded and unwanted.
ALKMENE: I just don't know—
AMPHITRYON: No, my Alkmene
Forgive me. With your words you've poured
Cold water on my passion's flames.   800
Since I have left you, you have never
Cast even hasty glances at the sun disk.
Here you did not perceive the moving wings of time,
And amid rustling pleasures in this palace
Fully five cycles of the moon have fled away
Like five mere moments in your estimation.
ALKMENE: I find it difficult, dear friend, to understand
The basis you may have for this reproach to me.
If you complain about my coldness to you,
I'm much embarrassed and at a great loss   810

How I should satisfy you. I do think, yesterday
When you appeared at dusk before me
I amply paid the debt to you, of which you would remind me
And paid it from the heart.
If you would wish for more, desire more,
I must confess my poverty:
I really gave you all I had to give.

AMPHITRYON: How's that?

ALKMENE: How can you ask! Did I not fly
When, to surprise me yesterday, you kissed my neck
As I was spinning—you had crept into the room—   820
Did I not fly t'embrace you, leaving all the world?
Can one more tenderly delight in one's dear love?

AMPHITRYON: What are you saying?

ALKMENE: And what are you asking?
You were yourself so unrestrained in joy
Of being loved so much; and, when I laughed
Amid my tears, you swore a strange and terrifying oath
That Hera never had made Jove so happy.

AMPHITRYON: Eternal gods!

ALKMENE: Then when the light of dawn began
    to glow
No pleas of mine could keep you here with me.
You wouldn't even wait for sunrise.   830
You leave; I lie down on the bed;
The morning's hot I cannot sleep;
I'm too aroused; I go to make an off'ring to the gods
And, in the courtyard, I run into you!
I think indeed you owe me an accounting
For your surprising presence here;
I am surprised, taken aback; I do admit it.
But that's no reason for reproaches nor for anger.

AMPHITRYON: Was it perhaps a dream t'announce my coming?
Did you receive me in your sleep, Alkmene,   840
So that you think you've satisfied my love?

ALKMENE: Amphitryon, can it be, an evil demon has

Deprived you of your memory? Or has
A god confused your cheerful mood
So that you would denude the chaste love of your wife
Of all propriety and jeer at it?
AMPHITRYON: How's that? You dare to state that yesterday
I stealthily came here at dusk?
That teasingly your neck I—hell!
ALKMENE: How's that? You dare deny that yesterday   850
You came here stealthily at dusk?
That you made use of ev'ry liberty
Which is allowed my husband?
AMPHITRYON: You're joking! Now let's be serious again
For this joke is unseemly.
ALKMENE: You're joking. Let's be serious again
For brutal is this joke and in bad taste.
AMPHITRYON: You state that I made use of ev'ry liberty
Which is allowed your husband?
Is that right?
ALKMENE: Be off, low-minded creature.   860
AMPHITRYON: Oh heavens! What a blow this is!—Sosias!
My friend!
SOSIAS: She needs five grains of hellebore.
There's something wrong up in her head.
AMPHITRYON: Alkmene! By all the gods! You have not thought
About the consequences of our talk.
Come, pull yourself together! Think a minute.
I promise to believe whate'er you'll say.
ALKMENE: Whate'er the consequence may be, Amphitryon,
I want you to believe me. You are not to think
Me capable of such indecent jokes.   870
You see me very calm about the outcome.
If you can honestly deny to me
That you were in the palace yesterday,
If then the gods don't strike you dead,
All other things are matters of indiff'rence to me.
You can't destroy my inner harmony,

Nor the esteem the whole world has for me;
I shall just feel a splitting pain inside
Because my dearest love does cru'lly seek to hurt me.

AMPHITRYON: You miserable woman! What language this! I   880
  s'ppose
You've found the necessary proof already too?

ALKMENE: I don't believe my ears! All of the servants,
  Your very palace, these are my witnesses. The rocks
  You walked on and the trees, the dogs who wagged
  Their tails at your appearance—all of them
  Would bear me out, could they but speak.

AMPHITRYON: All of the servants? That's impossible!

ALKMENE: Shall I then give you the most def'nite proof,
  Although I cannot understand at all why you demand it.
  Here is my final proof. Who gave this belt to me?   890

AMPHITRYON: What's that, a belt? You have it now? From me?

ALKMENE: You said it was the diadem of Labdacus
  Whom you had beaten in your last encounter.

AMPHITRYON: You, traitor there. What shall I think of that?

SOSIAS: Let me go on. These are just poor excuses.
  I have the diadem right here.

AMPHITRYON: Where?

SOSIAS: Here. (*He pulls a little box out of his pocket.*)

AMPHITRYON: The seal is still intact!

(*He looks at Alkmene's belt.*)

And still—if all my senses don't deceive me—
(*to Sosias*): Quick, open up the lock.

SOSIAS: By God, the box is empty.
  The devil must have stolen it himself!   900
  The diadem of Labdacus is gone.

AMPHITRYON: Oh, you almighty gods who rule
  This earth! What doom have you decided for me?

SOSIAS: I'll tell you all about the doom. You're double.
  Amphitryon of the stick was here before you,
  And I'd say you were lucky—

AMPHITRYON: Silent, rascal.

ALKMENE (*to Charis*): What in the world can make him so upset?
  Why is he taken so aback, beside himself,
  At seeing this, a jewel which he knows?

AMPHITRYON: Of wonders I have heard before,   910
  Unnatural phenomena which lose
  Their way by coming to us from another world;
  But here in this, a thread beyond our world
  Is fastened to my honor which it suffocates.

ALKMENE (*to Amphitryon*): Now that I've proved it, my
    peculiar friend,
  Will you still claim that you did not appear to me
  And that I have not paid my debt to you?

AMPHITRYON: No; but you must relate what happened in
  detail.

ALKMENE: Amphitryon!

AMPHITRYON: I said I didn't doubt your word.
  The diadem is not to be disproved   920
  But I have certain reasons to desire
  That you tell me the story of my stay
  Here in the palace now in great detail.

ALKMENE: I hope you are not ill, good friend.

AMPHITRYON: No, I'm not ill.

ALKMENE: Perhaps, it's possible, the cares of war
  Lie heavy on your head and, penetrating it,
  Have made your reason be their prisoner.—

AMPHITRYON: It's true, my head feels very heavy.

ALKMENE: Come, rest a little then.

AMPHITRYON: Leave me alone.
  There's time for that. My wish is, as I said,   930
  To hear report of my arrival yesterday
  Before I enter in this house.

ALKMENE: There's nothing much to tell. 'Twas dusk,
  Sitting there spinning in my room, I dreamt
  That I was on the battlefield, 'mid arms and warriors;
  Then suddenly I heard a joyful shout at the far gate.

AMPHITRYON: Who shouted there?

ALKMENE: Our people did.

AMPHITRYON: Well?

ALKMENE: I

Forgot it quickly, didn't even dream about the joy
The good gods had predestined for me. I took up
My thread again when suddenly   940
I had a shock all over.

AMPHITRYON: I know.

ALKMENE: You know that now.

AMPHITRYON: What next?

ALKMENE: Well, then

There was much talk and teasing and all the time
Our questions crossed and followed one another.
We sat down then—and thereupon you told
With warrior's words what you had done
There at Pharissa lately and that Labdacus
Had fallen by your hand into eternal night.
—And ev'ry gory battle scene you did describe.
Then—I received the splendid diadem   950
From you; it cost a kiss.
We looked at it this way and that in candle light
—And then I put it on just like a belt
Which your embracing hand put round my waist.

AMPHITRYON (to himself): Can one feel stabbed much harder?

ALKMENE: Then supper was brought to us
But neither you nor I displayed great int'rest
In the fine ortolan in front of us
Nor did we do much justice to the wine; you said in jest
That you lived on the nectar of my love.   960
You said you were a god and whatev'r else
Came to your head in your exuberant desire.

AMPHITRYON: —Came to my head in my exuberant desire!

ALKMENE: Came to your head. Well then—
Why do you look so gloomy, dear?

AMPHITRYON: And then—?

ALKMENE: We rose
  And then—
AMPHITRYON: And then?
ALKMENE: After we rose—
AMPHITRYON: You rose after your supper—
ALKMENE: We went—
AMPHITRYON: You went—
ALKMENE: We went—well!
  Why are you blushing now?
AMPHITRYON: This dagger penetrates my heart!   970
  No, my deceiving wife, it was not I!
  Whoever came in stealth last night at dusk
  Is the most worthless of all vagabonds!
ALKMENE: Abominable man!
AMPHITRYON: Ungrateful wretch and faithless
  wife!
  Leave me now, my restraint, and you,
  My great love, which lamed my justice;
  Leave me, my happy memories and joys and hopes.
  From henceforth I shall sate myself with rage and vengeance.
ALKMENE: Be off with you, ignoble husband that you are;
  My bleeding heart is torn from your affection   980
  Abominable is your artifice; it is an outrage!
  If you have given your affection to another
  If Cupid's arrow wounded you, and you had told me
  Decently, you could have had the same result
  As from this coward's trick you've chosen.
  I am determined, I can tell you that,
  To break the bond which pains your wavering soul;
  And, ere this coming night becomes reality,
  You will be freed from all your bonds to me.
AMPHITRYON: The insult I've received brings me such shame   990
  That that's the very least my bleeding honor could demand.
  It's clear that a deceit was perpetrated here
  Although my mind can still not grasp
  Th'accursed web. But now I'll call the witnesses

Who are to tear this web of lies to shreds.
I'll call your brother and my generals;
I'll summon now th'entire Theban army
With whom I stayed until this day did dawn.
Then I shall find the bottom of this puzzle,
And woe be to the man who cheated me!   1000
SOSIAS: Lord, do you want me to—?
AMPHITRYON: You just keep still.
    Stay here and wait til I return. (*Off*)
CHARIS: Your orders, Madame?
ALKMENE: You just keep still
    Don't follow me; I want to be alone.

SCENE 3

Charis. Sosias.

CHARIS: That was indeed a scene! He's mad
    If he can still insist that he
    Slept in the camp last night.
    Well, when her brother comes, 'twill all clear up.
SOSIAS: That was a heavy blow my master suffered.
    —D'you suppose I'll have the same experience?   1010
    I think I'll do a little prying.
CHARIS (*to herself*): What's up? He's got the nerve
    To turn his back on me and act quite peeved.
SOSIAS: Indeed there're shudders running down my spine
    Since now I ought to touch this ticklish question.
    I almost want to do without this satisfaction to my curiosity;
    It will not matter in the long run, after all,
    If one does not investigate too closely.
    Come on now, let the die be cast; I've got to know!
    —May heaven help you Charis!
CHARIS: How's that? You still dare to approach me,
    Bold liar that you are? You have the nerve   [1020]

T'address me boldly when I'm mad at you?

SOSIAS: By all the just gods, what's the matter, woman?
One says hello to one's returning husband.
Why get your back up right away and over nothing?

CHARIS: You say I have no reason? What do you mean by that?
Who has no reason? What's over nothing, worthless wretch?

SOSIAS: To tell the truth, I call that nothing
Which is called nothing in both verse and prose.
And you know nothing is approximately   1030
Like nothing, or at least not very much.

CHARIS: Would that I knew what now restrains
My hands. I'm itching terribly, can hardly
Bear the itch to scratch out both your eyes
And show you thus how mad a wife can get.

SOSIAS: Charis, for God's sake, what's been eating you?

CHARIS: You call that nothing then, that horrid way
You, shameless scoundrel, treated me?

SOSIAS: How did I treat you anyway? What happened?

CHARIS: What happened to me? Well look at Mr. Innocent!
I s'ppose you'll next maintain, just as your master did, [1040]
That you had not returned to Thebes before.

SOSIAS: As far as that's concerned, I'll tell you this
I don't pretend to be mysterious.
We've drunk a magic potion from the devil
Which seems t'have rinsed away whatever thoughts we had.

CHARIS: You think you can avoid my anger with this trick?

SOSIAS: No, Charis. Word of honor! May I be a scoundrel
If I did not arrive here yesterday indeed.
But I don't know a thing about what happened.   1050
The whole world seemed to be a great big bagpipe.

CHARIS: You say you don't remember how you treated me
When you came home last night?

SOSIAS: Oh, damn it all! I really do remember next to nothing.
Tell me about it. I'm good-natured as you know
And I'll admit it, if I misbehaved.

CHARIS: You worthless lout! It was already midnight

And the young princely couple had been sleeping long ago
When you were still there, at Amphitryon's palace.
You hadn't even had a look at your house.   1060
Then finally I had to go and look for you,
And what did I find then, at long last?
Where did I find you, heedless of all duty?
I found you lying on a pillow
Stretched out, as though you were at home there.
When I complained with mild concern,
You said your master had commanded this
So that you wouldn't oversleep,
For he was planning to leave Thebes quite early,
You made all sorts of lame excuses, just like this.   1070
And not a loving word, nor friendly one, came from your lips.
And when I then lean down to kiss you
As your loving wife, you, wretched lout, turn to the wall
And say that I should go away and let you sleep.

SOSIAS: That's very good, my honorable Sosias!
CHARIS: What's that?
  You have the nerve to praise yourself for that. I think you do!
SOSIAS: Really, you have to give me credit for that, Charis.
  I had been eating pickled radishes, you know
  And wanted then to keep my breath from you.
CHARIS: Nonsense. I never should have noticed it.   1080
  We'd had horse radish at our noonday meal.
SOSIAS: Is that so? Well, I didn't know. Then you would not have
    noticed it.
CHARIS: You will not get away with all this subterfuge.
  Sooner or later, all the scorn
  With which you've treated me will be avenged.
  It eats at me, I can't get over what
  You made me listen to at break of day.
  And, by my honesty, I promise you, I may
  Still use the liberty you gave to me.
SOSIAS: What was the liberty I gave you?   1090
CHARIS: You told me, and you were completely sober,

You would not care about a cuckold's horns;
Indeed, you said that you'd be quite content
If I had my amusement with the Theban
Who, as you know, does follow me around.
All right, my friend, your wish will be fulfilled.
SOSIAS: An ass told you to do that. I did not!
  This is no joking matter. I strongly disapprove.
  You will have sense in this.
CHARIS: You think that I can make myself.   1100
SOSIAS: Be quiet now. Here comes lady Alkmene.

SCENE 4

Alkmene. Sosias. Charis.

ALKMENE: Charis!
  Tell me what's happened to your miserable mistress!
  What's happened to me? Tell me. Look at this jewel.
CHARIS: What is this jewel, princess?
ALKMENE: It is the diadem of Labdacus,
  The splendid present from Amphitryon
  Upon which his initial he engraved.
CHARIS: That? That's the diadem of Labdacus?
  It has not got Amphitryon's initial.
ALKMENE: You wretch, have you gone mad?   1110
  It doesn't say, so you can trace it with your finger
  An "A"; a golden capital, and graven "A"?
CHARIS: It really doesn't, dearest princess. What is this madness!
  There is another strange initial letter.
  It is a "J".
ALKMENE: A "J"?
CHARIS: A "J". That's right.
ALKMENE: Alas! Then I am really lost.
CHARIS: How so? Explain, dear lady, what has so upset you.
ALKMENE: How shall I find the words, dear Charis,

T'explain what's not to be explained?
When, all upset, I get back to my room,   1120
Not knowing whether I'm awake or dreaming
Since the mad accusation has been brazenly advanced
That someone else appeared to me last night;
While I recall Amphitryon's passionate grief
And his last word that he would call my brother,
Just think, my own dear brother, called to testify against me!
As I now ask myself: could I be wrong?
For one of us is wrong about the other's error
Since neither he nor I can be a liar;
And as I now recall the ambiguous jest,   1130
I don't know if you heard it, Charis,
With which Amphitryon, my lover, uttered
The scorn he felt for the Amphitryon who is my husband,
I shudder then; stark terror grips me;
My senses all depart; and in despair
I reach, dear Charis, for the diadem,
Th'inestimably precious token,
My only undeceiving evidence.
I take it, want to place a kiss
Upon the darling liar's own opponent,   1140
And see a diff'rent strange initial
And stand there—struck by light'ning—
With this great "J" before my eyes.

CHARIS: How awful! Could you then have been mistaken?

ALKMENE: I, be mistaken?

CHARIS: I mean mistaken in this letter.

ALKMENE: Oh, you mean in this letter—maybe so.

CHARIS: And therefore—?

ALKMENE: What therefore—?

CHARIS: Calm yourself.
     It all will still turn out.

ALKMENE: Oh Charis!—I'd rather be mistaken in myself.
     I'd rather that the feeling in myself   1150
     Which I have had since mother nursed me

Which tells me that I am Alkmene,
I'd rather that a Parthian or a Persian seemed this feeling.
Is this my hand? Is this my breast?
Is that my image in the mirror!
He should be stranger to me than myself?
If you would take away my eye, I'd hear him still;
Without my ear, I'd feel him; would I not feel,
I still should breathe him; and if you take
My eye, my ear, my touch, my sense of smell,   1160
Leave me my heart; it is the bell I need
To find him in the whole wide world.
CHARIS: Of course. How could I doubt you, princess?
How could a woman err in such a case?
One may pick up the wrong dress or utensil,
But in the dark one finds one's wedded husband.
Besides, we all know that we saw him.
Did not the servants greet him joyfully
There at the palace gate when he appeared?
It was still day, that means that it's unlikely that   1170
A thousand eyes could have been darkened.
ALKMENE: And still this strange initial!
Why did I fail to notice then
This strange initial—not by the maddest brain
Is it to be confused with "A"—
Why did I fail to notice it at once?
If I have no discrimination, dearest Charis,
Between two names which are so very diff'rent,
Tell me, could they belong to two men
Between whom I could not distinguish either?   1180
CHARIS: But you are sure, I hope, dear lady, are you not?
ALKMENE: As sure as of my purity of soul, or of my innocence!
Unless you would misunderstand my feeling
That I had never found him as attractive.
I could have thought he was a portrait of himself,
Perfectly painted by an artist's hand,
Completely true to life and yet made godlike.

As in a dream, I don't know how to say this,
He stood before me, and a feeling quite inexpressible
About my great good fortune seized me,   1190
A feeling I had never had before,
When he approached me in the night,
Shining with glory all about,
The lofty victor of Pharissa.
'Twas he, Amphitryon, the god's own son!
It's just that he appeared to me to be exalted,
And I felt quite like asking him
Whether he'd just descended from the stars to me.

CHARIS: Imagination, princess, gave your love such visions.

ALKMENE: And then there was the ambiguous joke, my Charis,
Which kept recurring and distinguished for me   [1200]
Between him and Amphitryon.
If it was he, to whom I gave myself,
Why did he call himself only my lover,
The thief who tries to snatch a taste of me? I curse myself
For merely smiling lightly, and thinking this a joke,
If this was not my husband's mouth that said it.

CHARIS: Don't let such rash doubts torture you.
Did not Amphitryon himself acknowledge
Th'initial when you showed him the diadem today?   1210
There certainly is some mistake here, dearest lady.
If this strange letter did not make him doubt,
It follows that the "J" was always there;
Then we were blinded and deceived by our delusions yesterday,
And now today all is just as it should be.

ALKMENE: Suppose, he glanced at it but hastily,
And now when he returns with all the generals
And in a rage repeats his previous assertion
That yesterday he did not cross this threshold;
Not only would I be denuded of all proof   1220
But it now also testifies against me!
What can I then, confused as I now am, reply?
Where shall I flee from pain and from destruction

Once the suspicious men have looked at it?
I must admit that this initial
Is not the initial of Amphitryon.
Must I not then admit that this great present
With strange initial cannot come from him?
Indeed, if I should swear it on the altar
That he himself gave me the jewel yesterday,   1230
Could I be certain, tell me, that I yesterday
Received that same initial "J" from him?

CHARIS: Compose yourself. He's here. Now all will be explained.

SCENE 5

Jupiter. Alkmene. Sosias. Charis.

ALKMENE: My lord and master. Grant, I beg you,
    That kneeling here I give you back this jewel.
    Faithful to you, I place my life before your feet.
    If you gave me this diadem, look at it closely,
    This jewel with another man's initial,
    I'll gladly kiss it and my tears will fall on it.
    But if you did not give it, if you would deny this,   1240
    If you deny your gift, then let death be my fate
    And let eternal night bury my shame.

JUPITER: My lovely wife! Am I to take the diadem
    When such a precious jewel lies before me in the dust?
    Arise. What do you want? Compose yourself.

ALKMENE: I did offend you with the sureness of my word;
    But when I said it, I felt innocent and strong.
    But since I've seen this strange initial,
    I am afraid to trust my inmost feeling:
    I do believe—that to me—did appear—another man;   1250
    You merely need confirm it.

JUPITER: Heroic darling! How much you do shame me.
    What lie has ever crossed your lips?

How could another man appear to you?
Who could approach you, love, before whose soul
Only one face exists—that of your only love?
Saint that you are, you are protected
From any other with a di'mond belt.
Even the lucky man, whom you receive,
Takes his leave from Alkmene, innocent and pure,   1260
For all that comes to you must be Amphitryon.

ALKMENE: Oh, my dear husband! Can you now kindly tell me
Was it yourself, or was it not? Tell me, 'twas you!

JUPITER: 'Twas I, no matter who it was. Only be calm;
What you did see and touch and think and feel
Was I myself; who else exists, my love?
Whoever stepped across your threshold yesterday,
You only did receive me, dearest love,
And for whatever favors you bestowed on him
I am your debtor, and I thank you for them.   1270

ALKMENE: No, my Amphitryon, that is not right.
Farewell, my love, forever;
I was afraid that this might be the case.

JUPITER: Alkmene!

ALKMENE: Farewell my love!

JUPITER: What are you thinking of?

ALKMENE: Go, I say go!

JUPITER: Light of my life!

ALKMENE: I tell you, go!

JUPITER: Listen to me.

ALKMENE: I neither want to hear nor want to live
If I'm no longer innocent of heart.

JUPITER: My worshipped wife, what are you saying there?
How could a saint like you transgress in any way?
And had it been a devil yesterday   1280
Who came to you and had he hurled at you
Pestiferous slimy sins from hell itself,
He would have failed to mar the purity
Of my wife's bosom. What madness all this is!

ALKMENE: How shamefully was I deceived!
JUPITER: He was
  The one who was deceived, my idol! He was
  Deceived by his bad artifice, but you were not.
  Your feeling is infallible. If he vainly
  Imagined you were lying in *his* arms, *you* lay in fact
  With your true love, Amphitryon; and, if *he*   1290
  Dreamed of your kisses, *you* were kissing
  Amphitryon's belovéd lips. He feels the thorn,
  Believe you me, his loving heart is wounded by it,
  And no Olympian skill can free him of it.
ALKMENE: If Zeus would only hurl him at my feet!
  Oh God! We now must part forever.
JUPITER: More firmly did the kiss you gave to him
  Than all the love you bear me in your heart
  Attach me to you. And if I could
  Pluck yesterday out of the dance of hours   1300
  As simply as I shoot a bird out of mid-air,
  I wouldn't do it, dearest love, for all
  Olympian bliss and the immortal life of Zeus.
ALKMENE: And I would kill myself ten times.
  Now go! You will not see me in your house again.
  You'll show me off no more, to any woman here in Greece.
JUPITER: I'll show you off to all th'Olympian gods,
  Alkmene, that's what I would do; I'd lead you
  Into the illustrious throng of all the gods
  If I were Zeus. When you approached them,   1310
  Hera herself, eternal as she is, would have to rise
  And Artemis, in all severity, would have to welcome you.
ALKMENE: Please go. Your generosity is stifling me. Now let
  me go.
JUPITER: Alkmene!
ALKMENE: Let me go!
JUPITER: Love of my soul!
ALKMENE: Amphitryon, I've told you that I want to leave at once.
JUPITER: You think that I shall let you leave my arms?

ALKMENE: Amphitryon, it is my will. You are to let me go.
JUPITER: And though you fled beyond the distant lands
And to the horrid creatures of the desert,
I'd follow you clear to the sea's very edge 1320
And catch you there, and kiss you then, and weep,
And lift you in my arms, and carry you
Back to my bed in loving triumph.
ALKMENE: Well then, if that's the way you want it, I shall vow
And summon as my witness all the gods,
The terrible avengers of false oaths:
I'd rather enter in my grave than in your bed
While I have breath in me.
JUPITER: This oath I'll break, having the proper power,
And hurl its shattered fragments in the air. 1330
It was no mortal that appeared to you;
'Twas Zeus himself, the wielder of the thunder.
ALKMENE: Who?
JUPITER: Jupiter.
ALKMENE: Who was it, madman?
JUPITER: 'Twas Jupiter, I tell you.
ALKMENE: Jupiter, you say?
You dare, you wretch—?
JUPITER: 'Twas Jupiter, I said.
And I'll repeat it. 'Twas none but he
Who came to you last night.
ALKMENE: Forgetful of the gods, you dare t'accuse
The Olympian gods of consummated sacrilege?
JUPITER: I should accuse the gods of sacrilege? 1340
Don't let me hear you, thoughtless one,
Say that again with your mouth.
ALKMENE: I shouldn't say such words—? You wouldn't call it
sacrilege—?
JUPITER: Be silent now, I tell you. I command it.
ALKMENE: You're lost.
JUPITER: If you don't care about the honor
Of rising up amid the immortal gods,

I do: and you have made that possible for me.
If you don't envy glorious Callisto,
Europa too, and Leda, then I'll tell you
I envy Tyndarus indeed and wish 1350
That I had glorious sons like his.

ALKMENE: You ask me: do I envy women like Callisto and
Europa?
Those women glorified in all of Greece?
The chosen ones of Zeus, exalted women?
Who dwell in the eternal realm of æther?

JUPITER: That's right! Why should you envy them?
You, whom the honor of seeing but one mortal
At your feet completely satisfies.

ALKMENE: What madness are your words!
May I just grant myself the thought of it? 1360
Would I not perish in the face of such great splendor?
Would I still, if he had been here, feel in my heart
The joy of life? Completely undeserving
Of such grace, and sinful as I am?

JUPITER: The question whether you deserve this grace, or not,
Is not for you to answer. You have to bear
The fact that he did honor you.
Would you now undertake, shortsighted as you are,
To rule the god, who knows the hearts of men?

ALKMENE: Enough Amphitryon. I understand you well; 1370
Your magnanimity's enough to make me weep.
I know that you have said all this
For my distraction—but my soul returns
To its unhappy thoughts again now.
Go, my dear love, go, you who are my all,
And find yourself another wife to make you happy,
And let me spend the rest of my days weeping
Because I may not be the one to make you happy.

JUPITER: My precious wife! You move me much indeed!
Look at the gem that you have in your hand. 1380

ALKMENE: Save me from further madness, gods in heaven!

JUPITER: It's his name, is it not? And wasn't it mine yesterday?
Is not all that we see a miracle?
Was not this diadem still locked today
In its sealed box? And when I opened it
To give the diadem to you, did I not find
The space where it had lain, still visible, but empty?
And were you not already wearing it?

ALKMENE: Is this what I'm to think now? Jupiter?
The father of eternal gods and men?   1390

JUPITER: Who else could have deceived your feeling,
An instant scale and very accurate?
Who else could have deceived your woman's soul
Which comprehends so totally with sensitivity
As do the chimes within your heart
Which lisp their sound each time you merely breathe.

ALKMENE: The god himself! The god!

JUPITER: Only almighty deities
Would come to you as boldly as this stranger.
And I rejoice to have such rivals!
I'm glad to see that the omniscient gods   1400
Can find the path straight to your heart.
I'm glad to see the omnipresent come to you;
What's more, to have your soul receive them,
They too, my love, must be Amphitryon,
And even they must steal his features.

ALKMENE: Well, I suppose so. (*She kisses him.*)

JUPITER: Goddess!

ALKMENE: I'm so happy!
How glad I am, how glad to be so happy!
I'm even glad that I have felt the pain
Which Jupiter inflicted on me,
If all will only stay as pleasant as it was.   1410

JUPITER: D'you want to know what I think?

ALKMENE: What's that?

JUPITER: And if we have no revelation of it,
I still feel inclination to believe it.

Are you not always lying in the dust
In adoration of your love, Amphitryon?
ALKMENE: Alas, poor me! How you confuse me.
    Can instinct make one guilty?   1450
    Should I pray to the gleaming marble wall?
    I need to see a face to think of him.
JUPITER: You see. I told you so. And don't you think
    That such idolatry offends him. D'you think
    He likes to be deprived of your dear heart?
    He would not like to have your tender adoration for himself?
ALKMENE: I'm sure he'd like to have it. Where is the sinner
    Whose adoration is not pleasing to the gods?
JUPITER: That's true. And if he did descend to you,
    It only was to make you think of him   1460
    And to avenge himself for your forgetfulness.
ALKMENE: It's terrible!
JUPITER: Don't be afraid. He'll only punish you
    As you deserve. But in the future you will always
    Think only of the one who came to you last night
    When you pray at his altar, not of me.
ALKMENE: I'll give my sacred oath that I shall do so!
    I know exactly how he looks now
    And cannot possibly confuse the two of you.
JUPITER: Do that. If not, you risk that he'll return.
    As often as you see his graven "J"   1470
    There in the diadem, you will now think
    Most tenderly about his coming to you;
    You will remember the event in all detail;
    You will recall that, when the god confronted you
    There at the spinning wheel, a flash went through you;
    You will remember how you traded for the diadem,
    You will recall his help in putting on the belt
    And not forget what happened with the ortolan.
    And you will sweetly ask your husband
    To leave you for an hour or so,   1480
    If he gets in your way.

ALKMENE: Tell me about it, please. You frighten me.
JUPITER: What would you
  If you had roused his anger?—Don't be afraid—
ALKMENE: His anger? I? Aroused?
JUPITER: Does he exist for you?
  Do you perceive the world which is his handiwork?
  D'you see him in the shimm'ring sunset
  As it moves through the silent bushes?
  D'you hear him in the rushing of the water,   14
  Or in the splendid singing of the nightingale?
  Does not the mountain speak to you of him in vain,
  Although it points to heaven? Do not the
  Cataracts, dispersing in the rocks, fail in this mission?
  And when up there the sun shines on his temple
  And rung in with the pulsing beat of joy,
  All creatures laud him who is their creator,
  Do you then not descend into the shaft
  That is your heart—t'adore your idol?
ALKMENE: You terrify me with your words. Can one   1430
  Adore him then more piously or innocently?
  Has darkness ever crowned a day on which I did not
  Fall on my knees before his altar thanking him
  For this my life, my heart, and you, my love?
  And lately, in the starry night, did I not bend
  My head before him with deep piety while sending
  My worship, rising like the steam of sacrifice, to heaven?
JUPITER: Why did you bow your head before him?—Was it
  not
  Because you recognized in a great flash of light'ning
  Amphitryon's initial which you know so well?   1440
ALKMENE: You frighten me! How do you know all this?
JUPITER: To whom do you address your prayers at his altar?
  Do you suppose it's to the god up there?
  D'you think your captive mind can fathom him?
  D'you think, used to its own dear nest,
  Your feeling's capable of daring such a flight?

ALKMENE: All right. You shall be satisfied with me.
　From now on, my first waking hour every day
　I'll never think a single thought of you.
　Thereafter though I shall forget the god.
JUPITER: If moved by so much wish for self-improvement,
　Th'eternal thunder god were to reveal himself
　Right now in his full glory,
　Tell me, my love, how would you feel?
ALKMENE: It would be terrible to see him. If only I had   1490
　Thought of him more when I was praying at the altar,
　Especially since he resembles you so much.
JUPITER: The immortal face of Zeus you've never seen,
　Alkmene. If you saw it, your heart would
　Open up in infinite bliss. Your feelings for him
　Would seem burning fires; your feelings for Amphitryon
　Would seem like ice. Were he to touch your soul
　And then return to Mount Olympus, leaving you behind,
　You'd have the unbelievable experience
　Of weeping, that you could not follow him   1500
ALKMENE: No, my Amphitryon. Don't think that for a minute.
　If I could retrogress a day in time
　And lock myself into my room before all gods and heroes,
　I should be glad—
JUPITER: You would indeed do that?
ALKMENE: I should be glad with all my heart to do just that.
JUPITER (to himself): Cursed be the mad delusion which lured
　me here!
ALKMENE: What's wrong, dear? Are you angry? Did I hurt you,
　darling?
JUPITER: My pious child, would you not wish
　To help make sweet his infinite existence?
　Would you deny your downy breast to him   1510
　If he should seek it to restore his head
　Full of great problems and of ordering the world?
　Olympus too is empty without love, Alkmene.
　What good's the adoration of the people of the world,

Prostrated in the dust, to a love-thirsty heart?
He wants their love of him, not of his image.
Wrapped in eternal veils,
He wants to be reflected in a soul,
Or be reflected in a joyful tear.
My love, consider now how much joy he   1520
Pours out on hea'en and earth, joy without end;
Suppose that you were fated now to pay
The gratitude of countless beings,
All that creation owes to him, with but a smile.
Would you perhaps—no, I can not believe it,
Don't let me think that—let—

ALKMENE: Far be't from me
T'resist the great decisions of the gods.
If I was chosen for such holy office,
Let my creator dominate my actions.
And yet—

JUPITER: What?

ALKMENE: If I have the choice—

JUPITER: If you have—?   1530

ALKMENE: The choice, then he would keep my awesome
adoration
And you, my love, my dear Amphitryon.

JUPITER: Suppose then I turned out to be the god—?

ALKMENE: If you—
What's happening to me? If you turned out to be the god
—I don't know, shall I kneel before you,
Shall I not. Are you my god? Are you?

JUPITER: Decide it for yourself. I am Amphitryon.

ALKMENE: Amphitryon—

JUPITER: For you Amphitryon indeed.
But if, I ask you, I should be that god
Who's left Olympus for the love he bears you,   1540
What would you say to him?

ALKMENE: If you, my dearest, were to be that god,
I should not know where my Amphitryon was.

Then I should follow you, no matter where,
And though it be to Orcus like Eurydice.
JUPITER: You'd do that, if you knew not where Amphitryon was.
What would you do, if he were to appear now?
ALKMENE: If he would now appear to me—you're torturing
me.
How can Amphitryon appear now
When I have dear Amphitryon here—in my arms?   1550
JUPITER: And yet, it easily could be the god in your embrace,
Because you thought he was Amphitryon.
Why should your feeling then surprise you?
Suppose that I, the god, held you in my embrace
And thereupon Amphitryon, your husband, showed himself.
What would your heart say then, do you suppose?
ALKMENE: If you, the god, held me in your embrace,
And thereupon Amphitryon, my husband, showed himself,
Then I should be most sad indeed, and wish
That he would be the god and you   1560
Would stay Amphitryon for me, just as you are.
JUPITER: My sweet and worshipped creature!
In whom I laud myself so full of bliss!
So totally harmonious to the thought of god,
In form, proportion, string and sound,
My hand has not had such success in eons.
ALKMENE: Amphitryon!
JUPITER: Be calm, my love. Be silent.
All will turn out to work your victory.
The god is very eager to appear to you.
Before the stars begin to dance their round   1570
Upon the sky of night, your heart will know
For whom it beats with passion.
—Sosias!
SOSIAS: Sire!
JUPITER: Let's go, my faithful servant.
So that this day may grow more splendid,
Alkmene lovingly has made her peace with me.

Go now and summon to a feast for me
Guests from the camp, wherever they may be.

(*Both off.*)

SCENE 6

Charis. Sosias.

CHARIS (*to herself*): Oh wretched me, what have I heard?
  That they were from Olympus—they were gods?
  And that the one who seems to be my Sosias   1580
  He too, would then be one of the immortal gods,
  Apollo, Ganymede, or maybe Hermes?
SOSIAS (*to himself*): The god of light'ning! Maybe 'twas really
  Zeus.
CHARIS (*to herself*): I've acted badly; I should be ashamed.
SOSIAS (*to himself*): Upon my soul, he was not badly served.
  The fellow showed his courage and
  Fought for his master like a panther.
CHARIS (*to herself*): Who knows, I might be wrong. I must put
  questions to him.
  (*aloud*): Come, Sosias. Let's also make our peace.
SOSIAS: Some other time. I haven't got the time now.   1590
CHARIS: Where are you going now?
SOSIAS: I have to call the generals.
CHARIS: Dear husband, first permit a word.
SOSIAS: Dear husband, eh—? All right, I have a moment.
CHARIS: Did you hear
  That to my lady and her faithful servant woman
  Two great Olympian gods came yesterday at dusk?
  That Zeus, the god of clouds and sky, was here
  And that the splendid Phoebus was his escort?
SOSIAS: Indeed, if it's the truth, I'm sad to say I heard it,
  Charis.
  I never did approve of marriage of that sort.

CHARIS: Why wouldn't you approve? I can't imagine—   1600
SOSIAS: Well, if you want to know the truth,
  It is like wedding horse and ass.
CHARIS: Why horse and ass?
  A god and princess! (*to herself*): But I don't suppose
  That he comes from Olympus. (*aloud*): You deign
  To joke with me, your humble servant.
  A triumph like the one that's come to us
  Has never taken place in Thebes before.
SOSIAS: As for myself, it only did me harm.
  Shame, justly meted in a measure to me,
  Would have been just as good as the accurséd trophies   1610
  Which I must bear on both my shoulders now.
  But I must hurry.
CHARIS: As I was saying—
  Who ever dreamt of having guests like these?
  Who would have thought that in those simple human bodies
  Two of the great immortal gods would be disguised?
  We surely could have turned many a good side,
  Which carelessly we kept within, outside
  For them. We could have done more than we did.
SOSIAS: I swear, I could have used that, Charis.
  You treated me as tenderly   1620
  As a wild cat. You'd better change.
CHARIS: I'm not aware of having been especially insulting.
  Of having done more to you than—
SOSIAS: You weren't insulting?
  Call me a scoundrel, if you did not merit
  A beating as no woman ever got it,
  The way you talked this morning to me.
CHARIS: How so? What happened in the morning?
SOSIAS: What happened,
  Silly fool? Did you not tell me
  That you would grab that Theban whom I
  Have had to throw out of the house before?   1630
  You even promised me the cuckold's horns.

And shamelessly you called me cuckold to my face.
CHARIS: That was a joke, you know!
SOSIAS: A fine one; if you
Should dare to tell such jokes again,
I'll hit you, devil take it—!
CHARIS: My heavens, what is happening to me?
SOSIAS: That pig!
CHARIS: Don't look at me so fiercely
I feel my heart is splitting down the middle!
SOSIAS: Shame on you, sacrilegious woman,
For scorning thus sacred connubial duty!
Go then, and don't commit this sin again, 1640
That's my advice to you—and when I come back here
I want to eat fried sausages with cabbage, is that clear?
CHARIS: Just as you wish! Why should I hesitate,
Why wait another minute? It's the one, it's he.
SOSIAS: What am I?
CHARIS: Behold me in the dust.
SOSIAS: What's wrong with you?
CHARIS: Behold me in the dust in penitence before you.
SOSIAS: Have you gone mad?
CHARIS: It's you, it's you!
SOSIAS: Who am I then?
CHARIS: Would you deny it then?
SOSIAS: Has everyone gone mad today?
CHARIS: Did I not see
The flames of wrath leap from your eyes. 1650
Which are the powerful sun-god's rays?
SOSIAS: Me? Apollo? Have you gone absolutely mad?—
One treats me like a dog; the next one takes me for a god!—
And I am just the old familiar ass
Named Sosias! (*Off.*)
CHARIS: Sosias? How can that be?
Just that old ass I know so well?
You rascal! Well, I'm glad I know it!
And without sausage I shall show it! (*Off.*)

ACT III

SCENE 1

AMPHITRYON: Oh, how repugnant the faces of my foolish gen'rals
    Are to me. Each must congratulate   [1660]
    Me for the victory, and I must then,
    In turn, embrace each one,
    While wishing him to hell.
    Not one of them is so endowed
    That I could get my troubles off my chest
    By telling him about the jewel
    That was stolen from a well-sealed box.
    Now this can happen. A juggler can take a thing
    Out of my hand, although he stands far off.   1670
    But taking on a man's appearance
    And his manner and his complete connubial duty
    That is a hellish piece of Satan's work.
    In rooms lit up by candlelight, a normal person
    Has never been mistaken in his friends;
    Eyes, liberated from their sockets, even
    Limbs that have been severed from the body,
    Ears, fingers, wrapped in boxes, should suffice
    To recognize one's husband. From now on
    All husbands will be branded; they'll wear bells   1680
    Like rams. She is as capable of bad deception
    As her sweet turtledove; I'd rather grant
    The honesty of scoundrels who've escaped the gallows
    Than think my wife deceitful.
    —She's mad, and when tomorrow dawns
    I certainly shall have to send for doctors.
    —Would that I had the chance to tie the knot.

57

SCENE 2

Mercury on the balcony. Amphitryon.

MERCURY (*to himself*): Following you on this infatuated earth
    adventure,
    Old father Zeus, is proof of true
    Devotion on the part of Mercury.   1690
    By Styx! I'm awf'lly bored,
    For fooling the maid Charis as her husband—
    Perhaps deceiving more than necessary—
    Is not arousing of enthusiasm.
    —I'll look for an adventure for myself
    And drive him mad, that jealous fool.

AMPHITRYON: Why is the house locked in the day time?

MERCURY: Whoa there! Be patient now. Who's knocking?

AMPHITRYON: 'Tis I.

MERCURY: Who's I?

AMPHITRYON: Open up now!

MERCURY: Open up! You fool, whoever may you be
    To make such noise and speak to me this way?   1700

AMPHITRYON: Am I to think you don't know who I am?

MERCURY: Indeed I do;
    Whoever turns the handle of that door is known to me.
    —Do I know him indeed!

AMPHITRYON: Has every Theban had
    Some herb today to make him mad and lose his wits?—
    Sosias! Hey there! Sosias!

MERCURY: That's right, I'm Sosias!
    That is my name. That rascal shouts my name
    As though he feared I might forget it.

AMPHITRYON: Good gods! Don't you see me, you fool?

MERCURY: Completely.
    What's up?

AMPHITRYON: What's up indeed, you scoundrel!

MERCURY: What, in damnation,
    Isn't up? You tell me that and I shall answer you.   1710

AMPHITRYON: Just wait, you bastard. With my stick up there
   I'll teach you how you should address me.
MERCURY: Ha ha! There is a sturdy bolt down there.
   Don't be annoyed.
AMPHITRYON: The devil take it all!
MERCURY: Compose yourself.
AMPHITRYON: Hey there! Is anyone at home?
MERCURY: Phillipus! Charmion! Where are you all?
AMPHITRYON: That traitor!
MERCURY: I have to do your bidding, don't I?
   But you must wait in patience 'til they come.
   If you but dare to touch the knocker one more time,
   I'll send a roaring mission to you from up here.   1720
AMPHITRYON: That shameless, brazen creature! A fellow
   Whom I've often stepped on; whom I could,
   If I just wanted to, have crucified.
MERCURY: Are you all done now? Have you studied me?
   Am I now clear, now that you've stared at me?
   He's opened his eyes so far; if one could bite with glances,
   I should be torn to shreds by now.
AMPHITRYON: When I think what your talk will get you into,
   Sosias,
   I have to tremble. What beatings you will have!
   —Come on now, come on down and let me in.
MERCURY: It's about time! 1730
AMPHITRYON: Don't let me wait another minute; it is urgent.
MERCURY: Well, tell me what you want then.
   Should I let you in?
AMPHITRYON: That's right.
MERCURY: All right then. But you could have said that more
   politely.
   Whom do you want?
AMPHITRYON: Whom do I want?
MERCURY: Whom do you want?
   Damnation! Are you deaf? Whom do you want?
AMPHITRYON: Whom do I want? You dog! I'll break your bones

By stepping on them, when I get in.

MERCURY: My friend, here's some advice: get out of here.
You gall me, so get out of here at once!   1740

AMPHITRYON: Just wait, base creature, you will learn
How one treats servants of your sort
Who mock their master.

MERCURY: Their master?
I mock my master, do I? You think you are my master?

AMPHITRYON: And now I have to hear that he denies that.

MERCURY: I only know
One master; that's Amphitryon.

AMPHITRYON: And who's Amphitryon outside of me,
You blear-eyed rascal, who confuses day and night?

MERCURY: Amphitryon?

AMPHITRYON: Amphitryon, I tell you.

MERCURY: Ha, ha! Oh, Thebans, come and look at this.   1750

AMPHITRYON: Would that the earth would swallow me! Such
shame!

MERCURY: Say, good friend, tell me where the place is
Where you found drink to get so blissful!

AMPHITRYON: God!

MERCURY: Was this wine new or very old perhaps?

AMPHITRYON: Ye gods!

MERCURY: Why didn't you drink one more glass? You might have
Drunk yourself into being king of Egypt!

AMPHITRYON: All's over with me now.

MERCURY: Go on, dear lad.
You have my sympathy. Go sleep it off.
Here lives the Theban general, Amphitryon.
Go on now. Don't disturb his rest.   1760

AMPHITRYON: What's this? You say Amphitryon is in there?

MERCURY: That's right. He's in there with Alkmene.
Now, go I tell you, and be careful
Not to disturb the joy of these two lovers
Unless you want him to appear himself
To punish you for being brazen. (Off.)

SCENE 3

AMPHITRYON: Oh what a blow has struck you, poor Amphitryon!
The blow is fatal. I am finished,
Already buried, and my widow is
Already wedded to another man.   1770
What's my decision now?
Should I tell all the world about the shame
That's fallen on my house, or shall I not?
Whom should I spare in this? There's nothing
In my thoughts while I consider this
But the desire, passionately hot, to get revenge.
And let this be my only tender care
That the impostor does not get away alive.

SCENE 4

Sosias. Generals. Amphitryon.

SOSIAS: Here, lord, are all the guests
I could assemble in such haste.   1780
Though at your table I don't dine, I vow,
I do deserve the dinner.
AMPHITRYON: Ah, so it's you.
SOSIAS: Well, sir?
AMPHITRYON: You dog! You'll die now.
SOSIAS: Me? Die now?
AMPHITRYON: I'll tell you who I am.
SOSIAS: Oh hang it all! I know it, don't I?
AMPHITRYON: You knew it, traitor?

(*He draws his sword.*)

SOSIAS: Oh, help me now, my lords, I beg of you.
FIRST GENERAL: Excuse me, sir. (*Restrains him.*)

AMPHITRYON: Don't interfere.

SOSIAS: What have I done, sir?

AMPHITRYON: You dare to ask me that?—Don't interfere, I tell you,
  And let me give my rightful vengeance satisfaction.

SOSIAS: Before one hangs a man, one tells him why. 1790

FIRST GENERAL: Yes, be so kind.

SECOND GENERAL: Tell him how he has wronged you.

SOSIAS: Please keep it up, my lords, I beg of you.

AMPHITRYON: I'll tell you what this worthless creature did.
  Just now he kept the door shut in my face,
  Directing much abusive talk to me,
  Each word worthy of crucifixion by itself.
  Die now, you dog!

SOSIAS: I am already dead. (*Sinks to his knees.*)

FIRST GENERAL: Calm down!

SOSIAS: Oh, generals! Oh no!

SECOND GENERAL: What's wrong?

SOSIAS: Is he about to stab me?

AMPHITRYON: I tell you all, leave me alone. He must get his reward,
  A very rich one too, for all the shame 1800
  Which he just now inflicted on me.

SOSIAS: What wrong could I have done just now,
  When I have spent the last nine hours
  At the camp, just as you ordered.

FIRST GENERAL: That's true. He asked us to your dinner.
  Two hours ago he was at camp with us
  And has not left us for a moment since.

AMPHITRYON: Who gave this order to you?

SOSIAS: Who? You did, yourself!

AMPHITRYON: When did I do that?

SOSIAS: When you had made your peace
  With our dear lady. You were so happy then 1810
  That right away you planned a feast for all the palace.

AMPHITRYON: Ye gods! I must say, every hour, every step

Leads me much deeper in this labyrinth.
My friends, what shall I think about this?
Have you heard all that's happened here?
FIRST GENERAL: What Sosias told us is so little suited
  To being understood, that all you have to try to do
  At this point, is to tear asunder with bold step
  The whole deceitful web of this enigma.
AMPHITRYON: So be it then. And I do need your help.   1820
  Propitious fate has led you to me.
  I'll try my luck; my life depends on it.
  My heart is burning for enlightenment,
  And yet, alas, I fear it more than death. (*He knocks.*)

SCENE 5

Jupiter. Generals. Amphitryon. Sosias.

JUPITER: Who causes all the noise that forces me to come down
  here?
  Who's knocking at this house? Are you, my generals?
AMPHITRYON: Who are you? Ye almighty gods!
SECOND GENERAL: What do I see? My heavens! We have two
  Amphitryons!
AMPHITRYON: My'ntire soul is petrified with shock!
  Woe unto me! The puzzle has been solved now.   1830
FIRST GENERAL: Which of you is Amphitryon?
SECOND GENERAL: It's true. No human eye could tell apart
  Two whose resemblance is that perfect.
SOSIAS: My lords, this is the real Amphitryon;
  The other is a rascal who should be beaten.

  (*He goes over to Jupiter and stands by his side.*)

THIRD GENERAL (*pointing to Amphitryon*): Incredible! He's an
  impostor?
AMPHITRYON: Enough of all this shameful hocus pocus!
  I shall unlock the secret. (*He puts his hand on his sword.*)

FIRST GENERAL: Halt!

AMPHITRYON: Leave me alone!

SECOND GENERAL: What are you doing?

AMPHITRYON: I am about to punish
Deception of the lowest sort! Out of my way.   1840

JUPITER: Compose yourself. There is no need to get excited.
A man who worries so about his name
Can't have strong claim to it.

SOSIAS: I think so too. He's stuck a pillow
On his stomach, painted his face, and is
A criminal who thinks we'll take him for our lord.

AMPHITRYON: You liar! Your revolting chatter will
Be punished by three hundred heavy blows
Administered by three strong arms.

SOSIAS: Ho ho! My Master has a heart and he   1850
Will teach you soon enough to strike his servants!

AMPHITRYON: Don't keep me now from washing off
My shame in the impostor's blood.

FIRST GENERAL: Forgive us lord. We'll not permit this battle;
Amphitryon may not fight Amphitryon.

AMPHITRYON: What's this? You? You won't permit—?

FIRST GENERAL: You must compose yourself.

AMPHITRYON: Is that your friendship for me, generals?
Is that the aid you've vowed to give me?
Instead of undertaking to avenge my honor,
You would espouse the false side of th'impostor   1860
And hinder the just blow of the avenging sword?

FIRST GENERAL: If you could judge objectively in this,
You would give your approval to this step.
Which of you is Amphitryon?
You are, that's right; but so is he.
Where is the god, whose finger could point out
Inside which chest—they look identical—
There beats the heart of an impostor?
Once we find out who the impostor is,
We shall direct our vengeance, never fear.   1870

But, at this very moment, the naked sword
Could rage but blindly; therefore
It's better if we leave it in its sheath.
Let us investigate the matter calmly,
And if you really feel you are Amphitryon,
As we in this strange case hope, to be sure,
But also have to doubt,
Then it will be no harder for you than for him
To prove this to us beyond any doubt.

AMPHITRYON: I, prove to you—

FIRST GENERAL: And with most valid reasons. 1880
Without such proof we can do nothing.

JUPITER: Photidas, you are absolutely right; and the resemblance
Which does indeed exist between us
Pardons your wav'ring in your judgment in my favor.
I am not angry if you want to make
Comparison between myself and him.
Let's not decide as cowards with the sword!
I plan to summon all the Thebans here,
And in the throng of popular convention,
I shall make known my ancestry to all.   1890
He too shall recognize how noble is
My ancestry and that I'm lord in Thebes.
Mine shall he call the fertile fields of Thebes;
Mine, all the herds which graze upon the pasture;
And mine, this house; and mine, the mistress
Who dwells within it quietly.
And then the whole world is to learn
That no shame came upon Amphitryon,
And the suspicion which that fool aroused
Can be dispelled by me.—   1900
Soon all of Thebes will here assemble.
Come in the meantime and do honor to the feast
To which Sosias bade you.

SOSIAS: Upon my soul, I knew it.—These words, my lords,
Disperse all further doubts completely.

He is the real Amphitryon
Who now invites you in to dine.

AMPHITRYON: I call on you, eternal and just gods!
Can any man be thus debased?
I have to let the most notorious liar steal   1910
My wife, my honor, my dominion and my name!
And so-called friends restrain my hand?

FIRST GENERAL: Whoever you may be, you must be patient.
In a few hours we shall know the truth. And then
We'll not delay in executing vengeance.
And I say: woe be to the man on whom it falls.

AMPHITRYON: Go then, you cowards! Honor the impostor!
I still have other friends than you.
I'll still encounter men in Thebes
Who'll share my sorrow with me and will not   1920
Deny me help in taking my revenge.

JUPITER: Tell them to come here; I shall wait for them.

AMPHITRYON: You boastful scoundrel! You will in the meantime
Leave by the backdoor and get on your way.
But you cannot escape my just revenge.

JUPITER: Go then to call and bring your friends to me.
Then I shall say two words, but nothing now.

AMPHITRYON: By Zeus, the cloud god, what you say is true!
For, if it's in my fate to find you,
You will not say more than two words, you bastard,   1930
Before my sword's whole blade sticks in your throat.

JUPITER: Go, call your friends; I need not speak at all.
I can speak with my glances, if you like.

AMPHITRYON: I'll go at once, before he can escape!
Oh gods, you must grant me the pleasant satisfaction
Of sending him down to your underworld this very day!
I shall return soon with a host of friends
Who will be armed and shall surround this house;
Then, like a wasp, I'll press my sting
Into his breast, sucking his blood, so that the wind   1940
Will play with his dry bones when I get through. (Off.)

SCENE 6

Jupiter. Sosias. Generals.

JUPITER: If you please, gentlemen, do this house honor
  By ent'ring it.
FIRST GENERAL: My oath upon it!
  My brain is shamed by this adventure.
SOSIAS: Conclude an armistice with your surprise;
  Then go and eat and drink until tomorrow.

  (Jupiter and Generals off.)

SCENE 7

SOSIAS: It will be wonderful to sit down now
  And tell courageously
  About the war when others talk of it.
  I'm itching to report about Pharissa   1950
  And how we won it; and in all my life
  I haven't been this wolf-like in my hunger.

SCENE 8

Mercury. Sosias.

MERCURY: Where do you think you're going, shameless kitchen
    sniffer?
  I do believe, you want to stick your nose in too.
SOSIAS: Oh no!—I beg your pardon!
MERCURY: Out! Get out, I tell you!
  Or shall I fix your wagon?
SOSIAS: How's that again? Magnanimous and noble I,
  Compose yourself. Spare this poor Sosias just a little,
  Dear Sosias. No man can always bitterly desire
  To get into a fight with his own person.   1960

MERCURY: Are you reverting to your fav'rite trick?
   You want to take away my name, you worthless creature?
   You want to take the name of Sosias from me?
SOSIAS: Oh heavens, no! May God preserve me, able self,
   D'you think I'd be that stingy and that ill-disposed tow'rd you?
   Take it, take half this name; it's yours;
   Take it, that worthless thing; take all, if you insist.
   And though it were the name of Castor or of Pollux
   I should be glad to share it with you, brother dear.
   I don't mind that you're in my master's house;   1970
   But you must bear me too, and with fraternal love.
   And while those jealous two Amphitryons
   Are out to break each other's necks,
   Let's you and me sit at the table
   Peaceably together, toasting each other
   With our goblets and drink to their long lives!
MERCURY: I'm buying none of that!—What you propose is
      nonsense!
   Shall I then have no food?
   The table's only set for one.
SOSIA: So what! Since one womb bore us,   1980
   And we were sheltered by the same hut,
   And, since as brothers, we have had to share one costume,
   Let us then also eat from the same dish.
MERCURY: I don't know anything about communal life.
   I was completely isolated in my youth,
   And never have I shared my bed, my clothes,
   Nor even just a bite of bread.
SOSIAS: But we are twins, remember?
   You are the older one; I know my place.
   You will precede me everywhere we go.   1990
   You'll take the first bite, then eat all the odds.
   The second bite and all the evens will be mine.
MERCURY: Oh no! I need th'entire serving for myself;
   And what I leave, I'll save for later.
   By the great gods, what I would teach the man

Who'd dare to put his hand upon my plate!
SOSIAS: At least then, tolerate me as your shadow
    That's cast behind the chair on which you eat.
MERCURY: I wouldn't let you be my footprint in the sand!
    Get out!
SOSIAS: Barbarian creature! Man of iron,   2000
    Forged with a hammer on an anvil!
MERCURY: I s'ppose you think that I should now get out
    And lie down in the grass before the gate,
    And, like a journeyman, draw strength from the blue air?
    By God! There is no horse in all this world
    Who's earned a good meal as I have today.
    Was it not night when I arrived from camp?
    And, in the morning, was I not sent back
    To scrounge up dinner guests?
    And on these hellish trips, did I not wear   2010
    These poor old busy legs of mine down to my hips?
    We're having sausage now and warmed up cabbage,
    Just what I need for my refreshment!
SOSIAS: You're right; besides one runs the risk,
    Making one's way through all those forest roots,
    Of breaking one's right leg, or, even worse, one's neck!
MERCURY: Well, there you are!
SOSIAS: Poor me, deserted by the gods!
    So Charis has some sausage—?
MERCURY: Fresh sausages, at that.
    But they are not for you. A pig was killed.
    And I have made my peace with Charis.   2020
SOSIAS: That's very good. Well, then I guess I'll bury myself
    now. Cabbage, you say?
MERCURY: That's right. Warmed up, at that. And anyone
    Whose mouth is wat'ring now, had best be careful,
    Lest I and Charis should get after him.
SOSIAS: For all I care, eat cabbage 'til you choke, you gluttons.
    You think I need your sausage? The God who feeds the birds
    Up in the sky, will not, I think, let me,

Old honest Sosias, starve,

MERCURY: You dare to give yourself that name you liar?
  Base bastard, you would dare—!

SOSIAS: Oh no! I didn't mean myself.
  I spoke of an old relative named Sosias   [2030]
  Who used to work here formerly,
  Who used to beat up all the other servants,
  Until, one day, a fellow who seemed to drop down from
    the sky,
  Chucked him out of the house at dinner time.

MERCURY: Take care, I tell you; don't say any more.
  Take care, I tell you, if you want to keep on
  Counting yourself among the living.

SOSIAS (to himself): How I would throw you, if I dared,
  You scoundrel who are illegitimate,   2040
  And swollen up with brazen arrogance.

MERCURY: What did you say?

SOSIAS: Me?

MERCURY: I thought you had said something—?

SOSIAS: Who, me?

MERCURY: Yes, you.

SOSIAS: I didn't make a sound.

MERCURY: It seemed to me
  You mentioned the word *throw*
  And something else like *illegitimate*.

SOSIAS: It must have been a parrot then.
  They chatter when it doesn't rain.

MERCURY: Maybe that's so.
  Go and fare well now. If your back should itch,
  You may, however, ask about me here. (*Off.*)

SCENE 9

SOSIAS: You boastful devil! I do hope the pig   2050
  They killed will be your death!

—So, "he would teach the man who'd dare to touch his plate!"—
I'd rather share the dinner of a shepherd dog
Than eat from the same dish with him.
He'd let his father starve to death,
He would not even give the old man
What sticks between his carious chewing teeth.
—Go on! You merit this for your desertion.
Had I one sausage in each hand now,
I would not take a bite from either of them.   2060
How could I thus desert my poor, good master
Whom stronger might expelled from his own house!
—There he comes with his trusty friends.
—Another crowd approaches from that side! What's up?

SCENE 10

Amphitryon with officers, from one side. Thebans, from the other.

AMPHITRYON: Greetings to you, my friends! Who called you here?

ONE OF THE THEBANS: Heralds announced all through the city
That we should meet here at the palace.

AMPHITRYON: Heralds were sent? And to what purpose?

THE SAME THEBAN: We have been summoned to be witnesses
When your mouth utters the decisive word   2070
To solve the puzzle that has been upsetting
To all the city.

AMPHITRYON (*to the officers*): How arrogant he is!
Can you conceive of greater shamelessness?

SECOND OFFICER: He will appear too, in the end.

AMPHITRYON: He's very likely to.

FIRST OFFICER: Don't be concerned about it. Argatiphontidas
Is with you. Once I subject him to my scrutiny,
His life will balance on my sword's tip.

AMPHITRYON (*to the Thebans*): Hear me now, men of Thebes!

I have not summoned you,
Although your gath'ring here in throngs   2080
Is very welcome to me. He called you here,
The liar straight from hell, who wants
To drive me out of Thebes and from Alkmene's love
And to remove me from the mem'ry of the world,
And, if he could, he'd take the strength from my own
    consciousness.
Therefore, collect your wits, good men,
And though you be like Argus, each of you, and thousand-
    eyed,
Sent out at midnight to detect a cricket
By seeking out its footprints in the sand,
Still, don't spare any effort in this matter;   2090
But open up your eyes as wide as moles
Who blindly seek the sun at noontime.
Throw all your glances in a mirror
And turn its brightness fully onto me,
Reflecting me from head to foot in it.
And only then speak, give me an accounting, tell me:
Who am I?

THE THEBANS: Who you are? Amphitryon, of course!

AMPHITRYON: All right, Amphitryon. You said it.
When that damn son of darkness now appears,
That monstrous man, whose every hair curls just like mine;
And when your wits, confused by his deception,   [2100]
Lack all the signs that mothers need
To recognize their youngest children;
When you must then decide between us,
—Two drops of water would not be more difficult to tell apart—
One of us sweet, pure, genuine, and made of silver;
The other one is poison, lies, cunning, murder, death:
Then, citizens of Thebes, you must recall
Amphitryon am I.
And to remind you I shall bend my helmet plume.   2110

THE THEBANS: What are you doing? Leave that plume intact

While you stand in your prime before us.
SECOND OFFICER: D'you think that we would ever—?
AMPHITRYON: Don't interfere, my friends.
   I'm fully rational and know what I am doing.
FIRST OFFICER: Do as you like. But I must say, I hope
   You didn't do that silly thing for me.
   So what, if all your generals did waver
   To see that fool? This doesn't mean at all
   That I, Argatiphontidas, would waver too.
   If we are needed by a friend whose honor is at stake,   2120
   We should just put the helmet o'er the eyes
   And make attack upon our friend's opponent.
   To listen to th'opponents bragging first
   May suit old women; as for me, however,
   I much prefer making short work of things;
   In such a case one starts by running
   One's sword immediately right through
   The friend's opponent without any nonsense.
   So, in a word, Argatiphontidas
   Will show his pluck today,   2130
   And, by the god of war, no hand but mine
   Shall make that scoundrel bite the dust.
AMPHITRYON: Let's go then.
SOSIAS: First, let me kneel before you,
   My noble, genuine, though persecuted lord.
   I've fin'lly come to understand completely
   And now am ready for my punishment.
   Hit, beat and push me, step on me and box my ears,
   Kill me, upon my soul, I'll not object.
AMPHITRYON: Get up. What's happened?
SOSIAS: Of the dinner served
   They didn't even let me get a sniff.   2140
   The other I, who serves the other You
   Was totally bedeviled once again.
   In short, I guess I've been desosiasized
   Just as you've been deamphitryonized.

AMPHITRYON: You've heard it, citizens of Thebes.

SOSIAS: Yes, citizens,
This is the real Amphitryon;
While the one sitting at the table
Deserves to serve as food for raven.
Let's go! Let's storm the house at once
Please be so kind! The cabbage may be warm still.   2150

AMPHITRYON: Follow me.

SOSIAS: But look! He's coming and she's with him.

SCENE 11

*Jupiter. Alkmene. Mercury. Charis. Generals. Amphitryon.
Officers. Sosias. Thebans.*

ALKMENE: That's terrible of you! You say he is a mortal!
And you'd dishonor me by showing me to him?

THE THEBANS: Eternal gods! What do we have to see.

JUPITER: Belovéd, all the world must learn
That no one but Amphitryon, your husband,
Has dared approach your soul.

AMPHITRYON: Lord of my life! My wretched love!

ALKMENE: No one! Can you then change a lot that has been cast?

THE OFFICERS: By the Olympian gods! Amphitryon is there. [2160]

JUPITER: My dearest one, you owe it to yourself and me;
You must, you shall, my life, make yourself do it;
Come now, compose yourself; you'll have a triumph!

AMPHITRYON: By light'ning, hell and devil! Such a scene for me?

JUPITER: My welcome to you, citizens of Thebes.

AMPHITRYON: You murd'rous bastard! They have come to kill
you.
This will be it. (*He draws.*)

FIRST GENERAL (*stands between him and Jupiter*): Stop it!

AMPHITRYON: Let's do it Thebans!

FIRST GENERAL (*pointing to Amphitryon*): Thebans, I order you
t'arrest the impostor!

AMPHITRYON: Argatiphontidas!

FIRST OFFICER: Am I bewitched?   2170

THE THEBANS: Can any human eye discriminate in this?

AMPHITRYON: Death! devil! I rage, but there's no vengeance!
  This is the end! (*He sinks into Sosias' arms.*)

JUPITER: You fool, let me say two words to you.

SOSIAS: I swear, he cannot hear you; he is dead!

FIRST OFFICER: What good's the bent plume in this instance?
  —"Open your eyes as wide as moles!"
  The real one is the one his wife has recognized.

FIRST GENERAL: Amphitryon, dear officers, is here.

AMPHITRYON (*Awakening*): Whom does one's own wife recognize?

FIRST OFFICER: She recognizes him   2180
  With whom she's come out of the house.
  For what tree but Amphitryon himself
  Would she desire to be a clinging vine?

AMPHITRYON: Would that I had the strength to flatten in the dust
  The tongue that says that.
  She can't acknowledge him! (*He rises.*)

FIRST GENERAL: You're lying!
  The Thebans see it for themselves; you can't
  Confuse their judgment.

AMPHITRYON: I say again: she can't acknowledge him!
  —And, if she can acknowledge him her husband,   2190
  Then I shall ask no longer who I am
  And I shall say he is Amphitryon.

FIRST GENERAL: All right. Speak then.

SECOND GENERAL: Declare yourself, dear lady.

JUPITER: Alkmene, my sweet bride, declare yourself.
  Grant me again the bright light of your eyes!
  Say you acknowledge that one as your husband,
  And, just as quickly as the thought has struck,
  This sword will rid you of my sight.

FIRST GENERAL: Well, then. The judgment will be executed
  right away.

SECOND GENERAL: D'you know that man?

FIRST GENERAL:　　　　　　D'you know that stranger? 2200

AMPHITRYON: Would you then claim you did not know this heart
　　Of which your listening ear so often told you
　　How many loving beats it has for you?
　　You claim that you don't recognize these sounds
　　Which you so often stole with glances
　　From my lips, before you heard them?

ALKMENE: If only I could sink into eternal night!

AMPHITRYON: I knew that this would happen. Citizens of Thebes,
　　Peneus, rapid as it is, would sooner backward flow,
　　The Bosporus would sooner nest on Ida,　　　　　　2210
　　The dromedary wander through the ocean,
　　Before that stranger were acknowledged by Alkmene.

THE THEBANS: Could it be that he *is* Amphitryon? She hesitates.

FIRST GENERAL: Speak lady!

SECOND GENERAL:　　　　Say it!

THIRD GENERAL:　　　　　　Tell us!

SECOND GENERAL:　　　　　　　　Say something, princess!

FIRST GENERAL: If she keeps silent, we are lost.

JUPITER: Give voice to truth, my child.

ALKMENE: My friends, this is Amphitryon.

AMPHITRYON: *He* is Amphitryon! Almighty gods!

FIRST GENERAL: It's done. Your lot's been cast. Remove yourself.

AMPHITRYON: Alkmene!

SECOND GENERAL:　　　Leave now, impostor, if you do not want
　　That we now execute the rightful sentence.　　　[2220]

AMPHITRYON: Belovéd!

ALKMENE:　　　　　You shameful, worthless creature!
　　You would dare to call me that?
　　Not even in the presence of my mighty lord
　　Am I secure from all your raging?
　　You monster! More abhorrent to me
　　Than all monsters who nest in gloomy moors.
　　What did I do to you to make you come,
　　Covered by hellish night,

To spread your poison on my wing?   2230
What more, then that I, oh, you evil man,
Shone like a glowworm in your eyes?
I do see now what madness was deluding me.
I needed the bright sunshine to discriminate
Between the stature of a vulgar mortal
And the magnificence of royal limbs.
I curse my senses which fell victim
To gross deceit like this! I curse my heart,
Which spoke so falsely to me!
I curse my soul, which I can't even trust   2240
Not to forget her lover!
I shall flee to the mountain tops,
To utter desolation, where not one owl
Will visit me, if I have no protector
To preserve the innocence within my heart.—
Go then! Your despicable trick succeeded;
For ever is my peace of mind impeded.

AMPHITRYON: Oh miserable woman! D'you really think
    That I appeared to you last night?

ALKMENE: Enough of this! Now let me go, my lord.   2250
    You will be kind and shorten for me
    The bitt'rest hour I have had to live.
    Let me escape these thousand staring eyes
    Which, centered on me, hurl me down with blows.

JUPITER: You are divine! You're brighter than the sun!
    You'll have a triumph yet; a triumph
    That no Theban princess ever had before.
    And you will wait another minute.
    (to Amphitryon): Do you believe that I'm Amphitryon now?

AMPHITRYON: Do I believe that you're Amphitryon now?   2260
    You man, more terrible
    Than my breath can express!

FIRST GENERAL: You traitor! You would refuse,

SECOND GENERAL: Deny the truth of his identity?

FIRST GENERAL: Will you perhaps attempt to show us now

That the deception is Alkmene's?

AMPHITRYON: Each of her words is truth itself.
Gold, ten times purified, is not as genuine.
Were I to read what light'ning writes at night,
Or, if the voice of thunder called to me,   2270
I should not trust those oracles
As I believe her truthful lips.
I'll swear my oath on that upon the altar,
And readily die seven deaths
For the unshakable conviction
That he is *her* Amphitryon indeed!

JUPITER: That settles it! You *are* Amphitryon.

AMPHITRYON: I am!—
Terrible spirit, who *are* you then?

JUPITER: I am Amphitryon. I thought you knew.

AMPHITRYON: Amphitryon! No mortal understands this.   2280
Explain it to us.

ALKMENE: What kind of talk is that?

JUPITER: Amphitryon, you fool! Do you still doubt?
Argatiphontidas and Photidas,
Castle of Cadmus and the whole of Greece,
Light, æther, and all flowing matter,
All that once was, or is, or ever shall be.

AMPHITRYON: Come here my friends, come, gather 'round
And let us learn how this will be resolved.

ALKMENE: It's terrible.

GENERALS: What can one think of such a scene?

JUPITER (*to Alkmene*): D'you think Amphitryon appeared to
you?   2290

ALKMENE: Oh, let me stay deceived in this, for otherwise
Your light would cast my soul into eternal gloom.

JUPITER: A curse upon the bliss you gave to me,
Had I not to be always with you now.

AMPHITRYON: Come now and tell us who you are.

(*Thunder and lightning. The stage is veiled in clouds. An eagle
bearing a thunderbolt comes down from the clouds.*)

JUPITER: You want to know it?

(*He seizes the thunderbolt; the eagle flies off*)

THE THEBANS: Gods!
JUPITER: Who am I then?
THE GENERALS AND OFFICERS: It is the awe-inspiring god himself!
　　It's Jupiter!
ALKMENE: Protect me, all ye gods.

(*She sinks into the arms of Amphitryon.*)

AMPHITRYON: I pray to you
　　As I lie in the dust. You are the thunderer himself!
　　All that I have belongs to you.   2300
THE THEBANS: It is the god! We fall down in his presence.

(*Everybody except Amphitryon falls down on the ground.*)

JUPITER: It has pleased Zeus to visit in your house,
　　Amphitryon, and he will give a sign to you
　　To prove the satisfaction of the god.
　　Rid yourself now of your black care
　　And open up your heart to triumph.
　　What you, in me, did to yourself will never
　　Harm you, as far as I, in my eternal nature, am concerned.
　　If you will find reward in this my debt to you,
　　Then I can now depart with friendly words.   2310
　　Your fame shall henceforth spread
　　Up to the stars just like my realm.
　　And, if my thanks don't serve to satisfy you,
　　Then I shall grant fulfillment of your dearest wish,
　　And I allow you to express it now.
AMPHITRYON: No, father Zeus, I am not satisfied!
　　And I can now express my heart's desire.
　　Do for Amphitryon, I beg, what you have done
　　For Tyndarus: grant him a son
　　As great as were the sons of Tyndarus.   2320
JUPITER: So be it. To you there shall be born a son

And Hercules shall be his name; no hero
Of the past has been of comparable fame;
He shall be greater than th'eternal Dioscuri.
With twelve great tasks he will erect
His monument which will be indestructible.
And when that pyramid has been completed
And towers up into the very clouds,
He shall walk up its steps to heaven
And in Olympus I'll receive the god.   2330

AMPHITRYON: I thank you, god!—But you will not take her away
    from me?
    She does not breathe. Just look.

JUPITER: She will remain yours:
But let her rest, if she is to remain alive!—
Hermes!

(*He disappears in the clouds which have separated in the
meantime to show the peak of Mt. Olympus where the
Olympians are stationed.*)

ALKMENE: Amphitryon!

MERCURY: I'll follow you at once, my god!—
As soon as I have told that foolish fellow
That I have tired of his ugly face
And that I shall now wash it off my godly cheeks
With sweet ambrosia; that he has had some beatings
That are quite worthy of heroic lays; and that I am
No more, no less, than Mercury himself,   2340
The god with wingéd feet. (*Off.*)

SOSIAS: I should have much preferred to stay
Unworthy of heroic lays. In all my days
I've never seen so devilish a gift for beatings.

FIRST GENERAL: Indeed! A triumph such as this—

SECOND GENERAL: Such splendid glory

FIRST OFFICER: You see us overcome—

AMPHITRYON: Alkmene!

ALKMENE: (*sighs audibly.*)